Dr. Karry
Don Wesley

Dr. Karry Don Wesley

Reflections of a Life Well Lived

REDEMPTION
PRESS

Mrs. Cheryl Wesley, M.Ed.

Cover photo credit – Karl Wesley (son)

Published by Redemption Press, PO Box 427, Enumclaw, WA 98022.

Toll-Free (844) 2REDEEM (273-3336)

Redemption Press is honored to present this title in partnership with the author. The views expressed or implied in this work are those of the author. Redemption Press provides our imprint seal representing design excellence, creative content, and high-quality production.

ISBN: 978-1-64645-176-0

Library of Congress Catalog Card Number: 2020905894

This book is lovingly dedicated to our current grandchildren

Kamden James
Karter Monea
Kyrin King
Marlei Jhene

and to the others who will come forth in this generation and beyond, until the day of the Lord.

Your papa loved each of you and prayed for you every single day. He delighted in your antics and enjoyed spending time with you. You were his joy and the expressed manifestation of God's love for him in the earth. Always remember that Karry Don Wesley was proud of you. You are his legacy!

CONTENTS

FOREWORD

As I prepared to preach through the Book of Jonah, I built my war chest of study materials. I called my pastor and asked for copies of his sermon manuscripts on Jonah. He consented and offered to do me one better. When I arrived at his office, he gave me his sermons and a book by Dr. Karry Wesley. I thanked him. But he refused my thanks. The book was no gift. He was only loaning it to me. Pastor was clear that he wanted his book back. As I read through Wesley's volume on the runaway prophet, I understood my pastor's insistence that his book be returned. I quickly became a fan of the ministry of Pastor Wesley.

Some years later I was invited to preach a conference hosted by Dr. Wesley and the Antioch Fellowship Church. It was my first time to meet Pastor Karry Wesley. He was kind, gracious, and encouraging. After that day, I was privileged to spend time with Dr. Wesley on many occasions. He was never different than he was on the day I met him—kind, gracious, and encouraging.

The year Antioch Church celebrated its twenty-fifth anniversary, Pastor Wesley invited me to preach a revival. By this time I had relocated from Los Angeles to Jacksonville, Florida. I was eager to accept the invitation. It was my joy to preach that meeting each spring, until Dr. Wesley's transition to his heavenly reward. I looked forward to these annual trips. First of all, Antioch Church is a great preaching station. Some places invite you and expect a show.

Antioch comes together to be fed, not entertained. This is a testament to the text-driven and Christ-centered preaching and teaching the congregation received from Dr. Wesley over many years.

But there is another reason why Antioch Church was one of my favorite places to preach. The days I spent with Dr. Wesley were like being in an intensive seminary course of pastoral leadership. I learned so much just watching him lead, listening to his advice, and observing the strong congregation he nurtured. He was a great example, a wise counselor, a loving shepherd, a faithful preacher, and a kindred spirit. Conversations I would not dare to have with other friends, I freely had with Pastor Wesley, knowing that his thoughts about matters were guided and governed by the Word of God.

From my experience, there was no daylight between who Karry Wesley was in the pulpit and out of it. This was no more evident than when he went through his season of sickness. You will never see a greater example of mutual love between pastor and people. It was evident the Lord has placed Wesley in the hearts of the Antioch members. His beloved congregation was in his heart as well.

During this period, Pastor Wesley was scheduled to speak at my preaching conference in Jacksonville. He kept the date, instead of staying home for treatment. He preached the most memorable message in this history of the Cutting It Straight Expository Preaching Conference. Some of the great preachers of the country have preached this conference. But there is no comparison. In the preaching, we not only heard a man preaching a message, we also saw the message embodied in the man.

I thank God for the life and legacy of Dr. Karry D. Wesley. And I am excited that his dear wife, Cheryl Wesley, has compiled this volume to share his story with the world. May this book encourage you to follow the Lord, fulfill your calling, and suffer with joy to the glory of God!

H. B. Charles Jr.
Jacksonville, Florida

ACKNOWLEDGMENTS

Mʏ ʜᴜsʙᴀɴᴅ ᴡᴇɴᴛ ʜᴏᴍᴇ to be with the Lord on November 13, 2019. Four weeks later, I received a text from a longtime friend who asked, *Have you begun the outline on the book that you're going to write on your amazing husband, an authentic servant of God, the Dr. Pastor K. D. Wesley?*

My initial reaction (at least to myself) was, *No, I'm still processing his absence.*

But then almost immediately, I sat at the computer and began outlining this project by sections, chapters, names of potential contributors, and then the book title itself. In less than fifteen minutes, it was apparent that I had to move forward with this project that was alive within me, not just in honor or memory of my husband, but for the sake of our adult sons, grandchildren, and the other generations to come.

Because of our dear friend, I reached out to others who gladly accepted my invitation to contribute to this book. I am indebted to you all!

Thanks, Helen.

INTRODUCTION

How do you honor the life of one who walked before the Lord so faithfully? Karry Don Wesley was by no means a perfect man, yet he was perfect in his pursuit of doing what he believed God desired of him. He made some mistakes along the way, as we all do, but they didn't prevent him from continuing the path that was only his to take.

I want his legacies to know who their dad and papa was from some of those who knew him best. I want them to read narratives from multiple perspectives about Karry Don Wesley and what he meant to those writers. I want to give them the opportunity to review his life's journey through its various stages and to know the heritage and blood that flows through their veins. Even beyond these, I want our future generations to know the difference a relationship with the Lord can make in the lives of those who love, trust, and obey Him.

SECTION I

The Wesley Clan

1

Times I Will Never Forget

ALLEN "BUBBLE" WESLEY

I REMEMBER THE TIMES with my brother as having everything we needed at home. On sunny days we had a big yard to play in. At first, we only had each other—Karry, Brenda, and me. Before playing, the boys helped outside cleaning the yard and feeding the pigs, chickens, ducks, and horses. Dad always had a lot of cars in the yard, and as I think back, there was a large garden before that.

Our dad had a friend we knew as Mr. Tracy, who had a mule-drawn plow that we learned to use in the garden. After Karry and I removed all the rocks to clear the area, we helped till the soil and plant seeds. When we finished our work for the day, we would be treated to a ride on his wagon. We loved it.

Our first television was small but nice. Karry would let me know when the picture was clear. We really didn't like turning the large antenna on the roof of the house because we always got shocked. Most of the time television was all we had, so we would sit with Mom watching Billy Graham. She was our rock! There is no way any of us could have made it without her love and prayers.

Karry was always the first to do, to have, and to go in every-thing; that is, before me. He had the first birthday party, was the first to shoot a gun, the first to drive a car, and the first to go out to a club. Though I knew that we were under the legal age when we started going out, I followed him anyway.

During this time, Karry was hanging out so much that we wouldn't see him at home for days. He always had friends to stay with because he was the cool one. But I remember a time when Karry was home and some older white kids started calling us the N-word. Karry pulled one of them off his horse and beat the other boy in a challenge game of basketball so badly that he went home crying. I looked up to Karry.

One day Karry came home feeling some kind of way, but didn't stay long. He walked off mad, and Mom was upset. When I asked Karry what was going on, he wouldn't say. He was quiet, but I kept chasing him. I believe that was when he gave Mom the news about his calling to preach. You see, we didn't think God was taking him in that direction.

We didn't know for sure what was happening to Karry until one day we had a party for him. With a house full of his friends expecting to have a lot of fun, he walked in. Everyone started greeting him by saying, "Happy birthday," but instead of being happy, he looked sad.

He then said, "I don't want this anymore."

Confused, we asked, "Are you feeling all right?"

We found out that a so-called friend was trying to steal something. We wanted to fight him, but Karry said, "No, let him have it." We knew it was time to shut the party down. After that, my life changed as well.

Karry was a different person. His grades in school got much better; his focus shifted. Whatever Karry wanted to do, he did. Lots of girls wanted to be with him, thinking if they hung around me, it was a way of them getting closer to him. Those plots didn't work! I wish I could tell it all, but it wouldn't do him justice.

After I graduated from high school in 1977, the military and marriage were my next steps. Karry was now preaching the Word.

I had a daughter, Latasha Wesley, who passed away, and I asked my brother to perform the eulogy for me. That was his first funeral.

We did so much as kids—just looking back makes me smile—like playing in the pines, turning the rooftop television antenna, sleeping four to one bed, learning how to drive, having our first real job, and spending the nights at our grandmother's house. When I speak of playing in the pines, we were kids pretending to be adults, but not in the way some of you are thinking. Playing grown-ups for us was keeping a pretend house clean, climbing trees, and eating wild berries without knowing if they were good for us or not. At that time, being twenty or thirty feet off the ground in a tree was what grown men did. Karry was the only one who fell out of the tree! Thank God he wasn't up that high.

Swinging on the "Tarzan vines" was the real fun. As I remember the dangerous things we did, I know that God was with us. While swinging over dried-up ditches and ponds, sometimes the vines would break and we'd go down into a hard bottom or muddy water. We didn't break any bones, and although neither of us could swim, we were always able to get out safely. I was the heavy one, but still followed my younger brother on the vines.

Karry and I loved playing all kinds of games, like cowboys and Indians. You can guess who the cowboy was—yes, Karry! We also tap-danced with bottle tops under our shoes and enjoyed adventures while riding our bikes.

In our day, when Sunday morning came, we would get ready for church and leave home when we saw other people in the neighborhood walking. Dad and Mom came later. After church, Karry could be found carrying the pastor's bag. He may have been as young as seven or eight years old. Let me go back even before then.

Our dad's father came to live with us when Karry was maybe three years old. He loved spending time with Papa; we both did. We didn't understand then, but soon found out how important family was. Not long after coming to stay, Papa passed away. That was a hard time for us.

We all did our share in helping to feed the family. Chris was the hunter, Roy kept a job, and Karry and I were the fishermen. I remember one time we were going fishing, and I stopped at the liquor store. I asked Karry to go in and buy me a six-pack. He looked at me like I was a crazy man. Yes, I did forget about him being a preacher now. I wasn't at his level, but for me things just weren't the same. More and more, I started to have more respect for Karry's life and his calling.

If Dad or Mom wanted to go hear Karry preach somewhere, we were on the road. Sometimes he didn't know that we were coming. I will never forget when Dad sent Karry $1,500 when he was in college. Dad borrowed the money for him. When Karry came back home to visit, he brought the money back and said he didn't need it. I know both of them felt good about that. God stepped in for Karry and Dad. A lot of times you don't know who you can turn to but God and His favor.

When I think about when I got married, Karry and the family (Chris was a baby then) were with me. Man, that was a great day for me!

I think of our dad when he wanted to share stories and gifts with the grandkids like he did for us when we were kids. We rode horses, and the grandkids had a pony. Karry was the only one who could ride.

There's so much to talk about, but to make a long story short, God opened Karry's eyes to the days ahead and the people he would impact. We all looked up to him, even though he was the younger brother.

I know Karry's life was a hard road to travel, having to preach the funerals of family members whom he loved and would miss. Having the support of his beautiful wife and loving family didn't prevent these difficulties. I know it wasn't always easy. Everything we went through was placed there to teach us and show us the way.

Karry Don Wesley, I love you! I'll never forget who you are: my little big brother, whom we loved to follow. I'm going to miss you. You were the one who didn't tell us what we wanted to hear, but what we needed to hear—not just in catching fish so we would have something to eat, but to show us how to catch the fish so we could eat and feed one another. You always welcomed others in. Thank you for letting me in to learn some of what God shared with you.

Reflections of My Beloved Brother

JENNIFER WESLEY

M Y EARLIEST MEMORIES OF my brother Karry are centered on us in our family room watching westerns and football (Dallas Cowboys). This was a Sunday afternoon ritual in the Wesley household. Sundays were always set aside as a day for church, dinner, watching westerns, and, depending on the time of year, watching professional football or basketball. All my siblings were "Ride or Die" Cowboys fans, and if it were basketball season, rest assured we were cheering for the Lakers and the Chicago Bulls. Those were the prime years of NBA legends Magic Johnson and Michael Jordan.

Sunday dinners in the Wesley household were always a big deal. Our mother would always start preparing Sunday dinner on Saturday afternoon. Everything was made from scratch. The typical Sunday dishes of the day included some form of meat (chicken, pot roast, pork chops), candied yams, macaroni and cheese, collard or mustard greens, and hot water cornbread. Oh yes, let's not forget about dessert. One of the favorite desserts for all the Wesley kids, especially Karry, was Mom's chocolate pie. Other dessert favorites included German chocolate cake, banana pudding, and pound cake. Mom said the reason they called it pound cake is because the recipe required that you use a pound of butter. Mom would always bake her desserts at night, after most of the kids had gone to bed, to keep us from eating them up. Karry would often be the only child still awake, so he would have the luxury of licking the bowl.

Mom cried when all of her kids left home; Karry's leaving was no different. He was the first of thirteen kids to go to college and graduate with a four-year degree. When Karry graduated from Bishop College, he made sure all his younger siblings were present. This was our first time ever being exposed to a college environment.

I honestly believe that this was an intentional act by my brother. He wanted to show his siblings that if he could do it, so could we. Karry would continue to pursue advanced degrees and become a role model and mentor to his siblings, nieces, and nephews. His intentional act would yield amazing fruit. It inspired me to pursue my college degree, followed by two additional advanced degrees. It also inspired many of our nieces and nephews to earn their undergraduate degrees. My brother clearly understood the power of education.

Karry was the first in the family to pledge, or be initiated into, a college fraternity. I remember when my brother was the Dean of Pledges (DP) of Alpha Phi Alpha Fraternity, Inc. at Bishop College. This one particular weekend while serving as DP, my brother brought three or four students home for the weekend.

I'm pretty sure Karry was also scheduled to preach somewhere in our hometown that weekend. Well, they arrived at our house late that evening. Upon their arrival, I was sitting on the couch watching TV and falling asleep off and on. When I opened my eyes, the guys were reciting a beautiful poem that my brother had made them memorize. It was the most amazing thing I had ever heard. Karry truly had a way of making everyone feel special. I would later go on to be initiated into his sister sorority, Alpha Kappa Alpha Sorority, Inc. *Skee wee!*

I remember the first sermon that I heard my brother preach.

Honestly, I'm not sure if it was the first time I heard him preach; maybe it was the first time I started to understand what was happening. I was around thirteen years old, so Karry was about nineteen (he's six years older). I remember him preaching a sermon he titled "Pray at Midnight." Now I can't remember the Bible verses that Karry preached from that night, but I do know that it was this sermon that changed my life. It was during this moment of altar call that I would accept Jesus as my Lord and Savior.

Years later, when I considered myself a seasoned believer, I would often think about this sermon that my brother preached. It would prompt me to reference verses on praying at midnight. If I were a betting woman, I would say that his verse for that message came from Acts 16:25 (NASB): "But about midnight Paul and Silas were praying and singing hymns of praise to God, and the prisoners were listening to them." I would mention that sermon to him on different occasions, but he couldn't remember the Scripture reference either, understandably so—that was about forty years ago.

Another sermon that stands out to me as a child was a sermon that Karry entitled "The Pseudo-Intellectual Embalmers of the Supernatural," also known as hypocrites (Mark 7:6). He preached this sermon during a revival at Mount Haven Baptist Church in Camden, Arkansas. Our baby sister, Lashawn, and I still talk about this sermon. This was our first time hearing such big words.

As I conclude my comments, I believe that the biggest thing my brother taught me was to prepare myself so that I am able to take charge of my own destiny. For the last thirty years, my key message to youth and those whom I have mentored has been "Faith combined with discipline, education, and hard work equals success."

Faith + Discipline + Education + Hard Work = Success

I watched my brother Karry live this motto, and at a very young age, this is how I decided to pattern my life. Though I will forever miss my brother, I don't feel as though life cheated him. I believe that he achieved everything he set out to do, and I am so happy that he was able to see my journey in the military from start to finish. He was there when I graduated from college and received my commission as a second lieutenant in the US Army. He was there when I graduated from the Army War College and was promoted to the rank of colonel. And lastly, he was there when I retired from the Army after thirty years of honorable service. Thanks, brother, for sharing your best self with me!

3

I Remember When

PAUL WESLEY

I REMEMBER WHEN . . .

Karry had just started preaching and was being invited to so many different churches to speak. I would always try to go and support him.

We would walk from our old house down to the Ouachita River and fish from the sand on the banks. Karry would have his three or four reels all cast out, sitting quietly as if he was thinking about what his next sermon would be.

Karry was always by far the best fisherman in the family. We had many fish meals just because of him. He would never go fishing and catch absolutely nothing. He was the best.

One day Karry and I were on our way back from the grocery store where we had a credit account. We were in our dad's pickup truck, and Karry was driving when we realized that the door on the passenger side would not close. I had to pull and hold it securely to keep it from opening. On the way back home, Karry made a left turn onto Gravel Pit Road, and I flew out of the truck, hit the pavement, and rolled over three or four times! Karry halted and got out of the truck to make sure that I wasn't hurt. I promised him that I wouldn't tell Mama or Daddy what happened so that he wouldn't get into any trouble. They never knew. That's how close we were.

My wife, Cheryl, had our first son, Marcus. Karry and his wife, Cheryl, blessed us with tons of baby clothes.

Karry would always bring me some Dallas Cowboys souvenirs from college.

My brother Karry, when in school, always ran for a class officer position: president or parliamentarian.

Karry won the local "Rubberband Man" dance contest. This inspired me to be a dancer also and enter dance contests.

As I grew older and experienced more of life, I accepted Christ and later committed myself to preaching the gospel, just like my big brother Karry.

4

My Uncle Karry Wesley: His Life, His Family, His Faith

ANGELA DANIELS

Let me start off by sharing our family background. My grandparents Annie and Henry Wesley Sr. had thirteen children. They had three sets of kids according to age ranges (older, middle, and younger set). Karry was at the beginning of the younger set of kids. As one of the few older grandchildren, I grew up with the younger set of children. So I grew up with Karry more like a big brother than an uncle because he was still in the household when I was always staying at my grandparents'.

I remember Karry's first sermon that he preached at the age of fifteen years old at Zion Hill Baptist Church in Camden, Arkansas. God called Karry like Jesus called Peter. "'Come, follow me,' Jesus said, 'and I will send you out to fish for people'" (Matthew 4:19 NIV).

I was there when Karry brought a caravan of ministers from Bishop College (Dallas, TX) to Camden to preach a revival. This was a really big thing in our small town of Camden because we had not had a revival of this magnitude before, and it was the talk of the town. I remember some of the ministers staying at different houses of family members, including ours. I was impressed that Karry had planned the revival, got approximately twelve ministers to drive from Dallas, about 260 miles, and coordinated lodging for these young men. Who knew that he would collaborate with some of these same men ("The Bishop Five") years later to help keep the doors of Bishop College open? He knew that "the harvest is plentiful but the workers are few" (Matthew 9:37 NIV), and he was truly one of God's disciples.

In 1996, I had the privilege to move to Dallas near my uncle and his family, and I loved to be able to see them on a regular basis. It was during this season that the dynamics of our relationship changed. I was blessed to have him as my pastor for several years when I was a member of Antioch. Under his spiritual leadership was the first time I had been taught the Word of God. He helped me to grow spiritually, which is the most precious gift. When preaching, he always said, "Go back and read the entire chapter" of the Scripture reference for his sermon. His preaching would always make me want to read the Word to get more and to go back and see how he got his points for his sermons.

Also, I remember being at Karry's house in the kitchen having a conversation with him and another family member. Suddenly he said, "Angie, you didn't used to call me Uncle Karry. What changed?" I told him that I wanted Maya, my daughter, to address him as Uncle Karry, and I explained I had to lead by example.

There was another pivotal point in my life that also changed our relationship—when I lost my mother (his sister), Annie L. Jones. I immediately called my Uncle Karry while at the hospital because I needed some guidance. He helped me to make some difficult decisions. I remember calling Uncle Karry after leaving the hospital to ask if he would do the eulogy. I knew how difficult her loss was for me, him, and so many others, but I knew he was the one who had to do it. I knew that God would use him to preach an amazing sermon that would lift everyone's spirit. His sermon was so powerful and encouraging that it had everyone on their feet shouting and praising the Lord. His sermon gave me the peace (Philippians 4:7) I needed to bury my mother. I remember after he finished his sermon, he went back to his seat and sobbed. My heart felt for him because I knew they had a really close relationship. Later, I continued to reach out to him to get advice and guidance as I was battling intense opposition while handling my mom's estate.

He was the brother who sent his sister Annie roses every year for her birthday until her death. He was the son who brought his father to live with him and his family to take care of him until his death. He was the brother, cousin, and nephew who built a deck in his backyard so his family could have a place to gather for holidays and family reunions. He was the uncle who would keep his great nephew for the summer so he could pour into him during a difficult time in the nephew's life. Karry Don Wesley was a man of God who used God's platform to help people know the Lord through his preaching God's Word. He also used God's platform to help people build their own ministries. He was modest and helped so many people behind the scenes without people knowing it. He was a humble servant. He liked to be home wearing his comfortable jogging pants and T-shirts. He loved his roots, his childhood, and most of all, he loved his family.

When I look back at my relationship with my Uncle Karry and his impact on my life, I know that I am blessed to have had him in my life from different aspects (big brother, pastor, and uncle). Although I miss him tremendously, it gives me comfort to know that he's no longer suffering, and the Lord took him on the same date as he took my mother (November 13). I know they're all together with Jesus and rejoicing with other family members. I believe the Scripture Uncle Karry gave me to use for my mom's headstone is how God sees his death: "Precious in the sight of the Lord is the death of his faithful servants" (Psalm 116:15 NIV).

5

My Uncle, My Teacher

SHELBY GREEN

As a preschooler, I had fond memories of Uncle Karry. Grandma (Annie Mae Wesley) making chocolate pies meant only one thing to me—Uncle Karry was coming home from college! I would be so excited to see him. When he wasn't carrying me around, I was following him. On his visits, he sparked my quest for learning. I didn't need preschool; my Uncle Karry taught me reading and math.

As I grew older, Uncle Karry's influence continued. While living the small-town life in Camden, Arkansas, I would dream of going to college out of state. My dreams also included Greek life. My Uncle Karry was a member of Alpha Phi Alpha Fraternity, Inc., so that meant I should be an Alpha Kappa Alpha woman. Seeing his reality let me know that it could be my reality as well.

As an adult, I have been blessed to have my Uncle Karry as a spiritual leader as well as my pastor. I have learned so much under his teaching. I moved to Texas with a damaged spiritual life, but Uncle Karry's messages restored my faith. His impact has touched every area of my life.

6

The Voice of Peace

KEVIN MORIAN WESLEY

GOD GIFTED MY UNCLE, Dr. Karry D. Wesley, with the ability to deliver powerful sermons. I remember the final days leading up to my dad, Henry Lee Wesley Jr., passing away. There was a moment when I could see that my father was in distress, and I didn't know how to help him. In that moment, I placed my headphones on him and played one of my uncle's sermons. My dad responded with a smile and was comforted from the sound of my uncle's voice preaching God's Word. I am thankful that my uncle, Dr. Karry D. Wesley, could give my dad that type of peace in that moment.

I saw how Uncle Karry honored his mother and father as I was growing up around my grandparents' house in Arkansas, so it meant a lot to me at my dad's funeral when my uncle told me that I had done "a great job" sticking by my father.

7

A Gift to the World

REV. ROY WESLEY JR.

To me, Uncle Karry was a direct reflection of what I saw in my grandparents, Henry Lee and Annie Mae Wesley. Growing up in Camden, there was nothing like visiting Gravel Pit Road to be with my dad's side of the family. It always brought my sister Tamiko and me so much joy to visit that part of town; we both looked at it as an escape from reality for a moment.

As a young boy, it was hard to tell which uncle was which because there just seemed to be so many of them. I would get confused because I had cousins who were around the same age as some of my aunts and uncles. During the holidays, I remember getting into what felt like the biggest circle ever to bless the food. Rumor has it that Wesley men always seemed to have the most extended prayers, but maybe they seemed so long because we were ready to eat the delicious food my grandmother had prepared.

If I had to pinpoint the first time I met my Uncle Karry, I would say we probably met at the chocolate cake section on the dessert table. He and I were both lovers of chocolate cake, especially while my grandmother was around.

My grandmother was so proud of my Uncle Karry. She would

always tell us how his congregation continued to grow. She would ask my sister and me, "How many members attend your pastor's church?"

Tamiko would reply, "We have about two hundred members."

My grandmother would say, "Well, Karry has five hundred!" with a big smile on her face. The next time we would visit, the question would be the same, but the number of members Uncle Karry had would have doubled. The last number I remember her telling us about was probably around two thousand members. During those times, Uncle Karry became prominent and very significant to me.

Knowing that he was a preacher struck a little bit of fear in me back then. In those days, I thought all preachers were mean. This was mainly because all I saw most of them doing was yelling and screaming from the pulpit. I thought Uncle Karry must have been the same way by default. One year on the Fourth of July, he, Aunt Cheryl, and my cousin Chris came to visit. I remember being so scared that I might do the wrong thing around Uncle Karry that I felt as if I was walking on eggshells. When I got the opportunity to be around him, the first thing I noticed was his quiet and calm demeanor. At this time, it seemed as if he was concentrating on something in his head. I'm sure he was pondering on one of his famous illustrations. Unfortunately, the first time I heard him preach was during my grandmother's eulogy. I was around ten years old at the time, and remember thinking, *I've never heard a preacher preach like this.* He caught my attention like never before.

One illustration stood out that helped me understand what my grandmother meant to our family. He talked about going fishing at one of his secret spots around Camden. He mentioned these lilies floating downstream, but he happened to notice one lily that wasn't traveling on that same path. Unlike the other lilies, this lily seemed not to be moving at all. He then saw about thirteen other lilies floating toward this one lily, and as they got to it, they would turn upright and find some stability. He became curious as to why this particular lily wasn't moving. He decided to get in the water and make his way over to the lily to see what was keeping it from moving. Once he got to the lily, it became clear that the lily's roots wrapped around a solid rock. By the lily having a firm foundation, it allowed the other lilies to find correction at that moment. What he was saying to me during that message is that my grandmother having her faith planted firmly in the Lord allowed her to stand. Not only was she able to stand, but she was able to help her children when they came to her for help getting things together in their lives. Although this loss was one of the saddest moments of my childhood, my uncle made a lasting impression on me through that sermon. I saw that he had a special gift, and I yearned to hear more. I came to view him just as the lily he illustrated. He was planted on that Solid Rock, Jesus, and we could go to Him to find help.

As the years went on, I didn't get to be around the Wesley family as much. I would still go by and see my grandpa, but there weren't any big family gatherings I got to attend. Grandpa would always share these great stories with me. I loved hearing those stories, which is why he probably told them to me over and over again. He would share how awesome of a preacher Uncle Karry was and that he had written a book. I was proud that I had someone in the family getting so much attention for doing the work of the Lord. I also noticed that my grandpa would have different vehicles in the driveway. It turns out that Uncle Karry was giving him cars. The last one I remember him having was a light blue Lincoln Town Car.

During the years of 2004–5, I had to do a tour of duty in Iraq with my Army National Guard unit. While I was gone overseas, I learned that my grandpa developed cancer. I learned that he would be going to stay in Dallas with my Uncle Karry and his family. When I returned to the States, I called my Aunt Jennifer. She told me Grandpa didn't have much longer to be here, and I should try to get down to see him as soon as I could. I talked with my Uncle Allen, who told me he planned to drive down to Dallas for a few days and welcomed me to come. We only planned to stay for a couple of days, say our goodbyes, and travel back to Camden, but during the trip, Uncle Allen's car broke down. We ended up staying there for the whole week. During this week, Uncle Karry was in revival in Oklahoma and wouldn't return until Thursday or Friday of that week.

I stood amazed when I got to my uncle's house. He had everything you could ask for or think of in that house plus a swimming pool and basketball court outside. I was impressed. Aunt Cheryl then took me on a tour of the church. I had never seen a church that big. I was excited about all the different ministries they had going on.

As I spent time with my grandpa during that week, I saw him going through pain, yet I saw him praising the Lord. I wondered how a man could be facing the end of his life and still hold on and trust God. During our one-on-one time, he expressed that he loved us all and was proud of me. He taught me a great deal about trusting God in those hours.

When my Uncle Karry returned home, it was the first time I'd seen him in years. I stood up, looked him in the eyes, and tried to give him the manliest of handshakes. Uncle Karry took this moment to extend some Wesley love. He pulled me in and gave me the biggest hug ever. I said, "It's good to see you."

He then said, "No, it's good to see you, nephew; we've been praying for you."

That made me feel like I was on top of the world, but it also brought me back to the reality that he was human and that he loved family. My grandpa transitioned that Saturday with family around the bed singing songs of Zion.

As time went on, I wanted to learn more about my uncle. I remember going to the Antioch website and watching Karry's Korner (he spelled it with a "K" like he was a Kappa), a series of videos where my Uncle Karry opened up about many of his views. One thing that stuck out to me was the order of importance he put on values in his life. He said to the interviewer, "It's God, family, then church." I'd always heard preachers say that it was God, church, then family, but here this man who had built this great ministry put his family before the church. I admired his heart for this very reason. Over the years, I saw him fully supporting his sons. Whatever they had going, he did his best to be there for them. I saw him travel to Charles's basketball games when he was playing college ball for Henderson State University. I got to attend a few of those games with him, and he was proud every time Charles got on the court.

Uncle Karry's house was where we had most of our big family gatherings. We surprised him for his fiftieth birthday party, celebrated Aunt Doris's sixtieth birthday, had a Heard family reunion there, as well as a Wesley family reunion, and I cannot forget the many Thanksgiving holidays spent at my uncle's house.

My sister Tamiko loved going down there to be at his home. It brought back old times to her, and she always gained a bit of strength and peace from going to spend those times with the family. She told me I'd better not ever go to Uncle Karry's house without taking her with me. She loved Unc a great deal. In 2012, Tamiko was in Houston going through cancer treatment at MD Anderson Cancer Center. We drove from Houston to Dallas one weekend so she could be around the family at Uncle Karry's house one more time.

It brought her so much joy to go and share those moments with our family. I know it made her want to fight even more. Uncle Karry prayed for her, and I know it gave her inspiration to keep trusting in God's plan for her life. As we drove back to Houston, she was ready to take on whatever came her way, and however things ended up, she had the confidence that God was on her side. She needed that visit. She needed those encouraging words from my Uncle Karry and the rest of the family. Although she didn't make it through that situation, her faith was active in the Lord. She passed away in February 2013, holding on to God's unchanging hand. Uncle Karry did her eulogy a couple of weeks after her passing, and I could just see her shouting in heaven as he preached the Twenty-third Psalm to us.

I preached my first sermon in August 2014. A few weeks after, I would head to Dallas to attend the Forty-niners vs. Cowboys game. Before making the trip to Dallas, I called Aunt Cheryl to inform her I would be in town and that I planned to attend church with them on that Sunday morning. She then insisted that I stay with them for the weekend, and I gladly accepted her offer.

Upon arrival, I took my things upstairs and got settled. Soon after I sat down, Uncle Karry came upstairs and had a "seminary session" with me. He gave me so much knowledge during those moments. Uncle Karry talked about how much I needed to study God's Word and that my sermon should come from the overflow of my studying.

The next thing he told me is something I will carry with me for the rest of my life. He said that the most significant sermon you will ever preach would be how you treat your family. He expressed to me that people are going to watch how you interact with your son and how you treat your wife. Those things are going to speak volumes about what God is doing in your life. He talked about how important he felt it was for him to break a cycle that was going on in our family, with some marriages not working. We make time for the things we love and enjoy in our lives, and he pointed out to me that he loved God and he loved his family. These are the values that were sitting right in front of me through him. He was that lily rooted on that solid rock. He was going to stick with God until the end. He was going to love his family through it all.

The first time I went to an Antioch service, the Spirit was high when we walked in the door. I saw people who weren't ashamed to praise God. It felt like everyone was engaged in the worship experience. I didn't want to leave that place. I was amazed by each sermon I heard him preach. He took command of the Scripture like no one I had ever heard before. He broke it down to the point that young children could understand, but he put something special in it that could get anyone out their seat.

He did a few revivals at the church I currently attend, and I felt excited to share the pulpit with such a mighty man of God. I had the privilege of introducing him each year that he came, and I was "peacock proud" to do so. After each night, he would hand me his Bible, and I would stand next to him as people would come up, shake his hand, and tell him how well he did. He always replied with "Bless you." He was so humble. He had just set the church on fire, but would give all the credit to God.

I looked up to him for who he was to our family and who he was to me. He motivated me to love and cherish my own family. He drove me to study the Scripture and to dig deep for examples of God's work in my own life. He was indeed a gift to me and to the rest of the world. I was just lucky enough to call him Uncle Karry.

8

Just a Country Boy

BRENDA JUNIEL ROBINSON

What can I say about my brother?
Out of all the achievements that he achieved in his life,
Before he preached his first sermon here at Zion Hill,
Before he became pastor, teacher, and evangelist of his great church at Antioch,
Before he wrote his first book,
Before he received his doctorate,
Before he became a husband, a father, and Papa to his loving family,
Karry was just a country boy from down there on Gravel Pit Road.

A BOY FULL OF curiosity, he loved being outside climbing trees, eating wild berries and sweet grass, playing in his daddy's old cars, riding horses, going fishing, and just doing those things that little boys loved to do.

He was also very mischievous; he loved to start fires. Mom called him the "little firebug." He would always set the grass on fire. We had a place where we liked to play called the pines, and he set the pines on fire. I mean, where did he get the matches? He was just little. I don't know where he got those matches.

He also loved to play jokes. He loved locking people in the trunk of his daddy's old cars, even though he knew he didn't have the right key to unlock the trunk. Mr. Henry had hundreds of keys hanging on the wall.

One day Mrs. Wesley had to call Mr. Henry to come home from work so he could get the right key to unlock the trunk and get whoever was in there out. And yes, I was one of them. He got me one time, and one time only.

Later, we called ourselves the Gravel Pit Road Gang, and you know who the leader was—Karry. He would say, "Come on y'all. I know a good place where we can pick plums, berries, and apricots," and he would take us way down off in the woods somewhere.

I would say, "I know good and well there ain't no plums down here." But when we got off in there, we found a treasure, because he knew where it was. And of course, sometimes we would steal pomegranates and pears off Mrs. Biggers's trees.

We would meet up on Sunday mornings and walk to church, where we would all be singing in the youth choir. Karry had a song he liked called "Tell It." The few words of that song said, "I'll tell it everywhere He blesses me to go." He would lead that song all the time, not knowing that, even at that age, God was preparing him to do just that. His ministry took him all over the world.

So before I close, I have to tell y'all this. The Gravel Pit Road Gang had a special sound, or a call, that we would make whenever we wanted to get together and play. We would stand on our back porch and holler across the field to the Wesley's, and they would do the same and holler for us. Whenever we heard that call, we would stop what we were doing—I don't care if we were eating or sleeping. We would just wake up out of our sleep when we heard that call and would take off running to wherever that call was coming from. Do y'all remember the Tarzan movie? When Tarzan made that sound, the animals would come to attention and rally toward Tarzan. He was known as the king of the jungle.

Well, the other day, my brother Karry heard another sound

that was calling him, and it wasn't Tarzan, the king of the jungle. It was the King of kings, the Lord of lords; He was beckoning him to come, and it got his attention. No matter how bad he wanted to stay here, he knew he had to leave. And because he is in the arms of Jesus, we do not weep as those who have no hope because, one day we will see him again. The Bible says, "We shall not all sleep, but we shall all be changed, in a moment, in the twinkling of an eye" (1 Corinthians 15:51–52 KJV). And it also says, "The dead in Christ shall rise first: then we which . . . remain shall be caught up . . . to meet the Lord in the air" (1 Thessalonians 4:16–17 KJV).

So I say farewell to my brother and God bless you to my family.

9

My Famous (Great) Uncle

MAYA DANIELS

THERE ARE TRULY NO words to describe the hurt I experienced when you left. You have been there every step of the way, always supporting me from the sidelines. I don't really know what to say other than thank you for the unconditional love and support.

I will always remember one time during the summer I was visiting, and I wanted to show you how I had learned to count in Spanish. I was counting, but I didn't know any of the numbers past thirty. Then about a week after we returned home, my parents called me downstairs because they had a surprise. They brought out my CD player and pressed play. Out came your voice explaining how I was there a week ago and couldn't count that high. I may not remember exactly what the sermon was about, but I will never forget feeling like the most special person in the world. Not everyone can say their famous uncle talked about them on his weekly television program! I also was mad at the time because I had learned more since I left, but didn't get to show you. I remember playing the CD over and over again just to hear you talk about me.

I was always proud of you and what you did, always taking any chance I could to brag about my famous uncle in Texas, the pastor of a church that was, in my words, "bigger than the whole city." It may have been an exaggeration, but I was young and took pride in it nonetheless.

You will always continue to have an impact on my life. I will hear your voice as I make decisions guiding me along the way as you always did.

Love always.

SECTION II

The First Family

10

My Honey

CHERYL WESLEY

It's hard to believe that my honey and I were married for thirty-four years. The funny thing is, I had not seriously considered marriage to anyone until maybe a year before dating Karry. My life was going well. I had a strong relationship with the Lord, had completed my graduate degree, was loving life as a young professional, was active with my sorority sisters, and enjoyed the company of great friends. I had even begun the planning stages of purchasing a home near Lake Ray Hubbard and adopting a child. When Karry and I started dating, everything changed, and quickly.

After two short dating cycles, Karry asked me to marry him in July 1985. I accepted his proposal, met some of his family members, and literally five months later, we were married. At the time, I couldn't quite understand the urgency of our union and inquired of the Lord several times. He gave me His peace, and we moved forward.

My honey and I believed God for a strong marriage and were committed to Him first, and then to each another. I would be untruthful if I said that we didn't have struggles along the way. We did, but we never argued. It's true, because Karry would not argue with me. I tried once early on in our marriage and felt like an idiot afterward because he didn't say a word. That is, until several days later. He began very softly, and in his calm voice said, "A few days ago . . ." Well of course by then, I had forgotten what I was angry about, and the fight in me was completely gone. We discussed my actions, he explained his position, and we made a commitment to communicate better going forward. That was it. We needed that plan in place to keep our foundation strong. We trusted the Lord. Only He knew the path that we had to take and the necessity of our combined faith to combat all that would come against us.

While many only saw the good things we were juggling—our new marriage, Karry's anointed preaching and servant leadership, his pursuit of advanced degrees, my unwavering support, and the beginning of Antioch Fellowship—only a few selected prayer warriors knew of the hateful phone calls, negative rumors, undesired advances to sever our relationship, and the many plots of external "church leaders" to destroy what God had ordained. We cried, we fasted, we prayed, we studied, and we encouraged one another. We trusted God's plan together and kept moving forward with the support of our amazing church family.

The people of Antioch Fellowship loved the Lord and supported Karry. He knew that God had given him the task of leading this people, and he was obedient to the call. They saw it, too, and obeyed the move of God. He was twenty-five years old when we began this journey, and they followed him. They prayed for him. They encouraged him and walked alongside. He was grateful and motivated every single day to lead them in love.

My honey was a genuine servant leader with a vision for the people of God. He led by example. No task was too menial for his hands to perform. No person was beneath his status to greet and embrace. He exemplified what the love of Jesus looked like. He shared resources with those in need, preached the gospel to anyone who would listen, and encouraged the body of Christ to take the message to the world in our daily lives. No one was beyond his capacity to love, and I supported him wholeheartedly.

Four years after our marriage, we built our first home and immediately started our family with the addition of our firstborn son, Christopher Keith Wesley. Karry was so proud to be a father. A year and a half later to his extreme delight, our second son, Karl Christian Wesley was born. We both agreed that two boys would be more than enough to handle, and we didn't plan to have any more children. We were now a traditional family of four. Five years later, however, that all changed. To our pleasant surprise, our "caboose," Charles Kenyon Wesley, made his unexpected arrival.

My honey was an extremely proud father who took his roles of provision, presence, and prophet seriously. He provided financially for his sons' needs and most of their desires. He made sure they lacked nothing, and I mean nothing. In addition to providing the basic necessities of shelter, clothing, shoes, and food, he also purchased all types of sports equipment, planned and paid for trips, paid college tuition, purchased cars, paid for insurance, and then gave them gas money. On many family cruises, the fellas were allowed to take a friend. Their father was an active participant in their lives and took pride in attending school programs and all their athletic activities. More than that, he was home with them (us). Finally, he showed his sons what a man of God looked like. They watched him love his wife in tangible ways, felt him love and provide for them, saw him read Scripture and pray, and even brought their friends to him when they experienced problems. He was their godly example.

There's much to be said about Karry's love. He delighted in surprising me with unexpected trips, cars, and gatherings. In the early years, he coordinated the dates for our vacations with my supervisors, and with family or close friends who committed to care for our sons. Then, with only one or two days before our departure, he would share the plans with me. I soon learned the importance of keeping an ample supply of clean outfits for all of us.

In addition to the trips, Karry enjoyed buying new vehicles. As soon as I would get accustomed to driving one, he would purchase another. I remember paying off my first car, a Nissan 280ZX. He took it to the carwash, and came back two hours later with a new 300ZX. That was the first of many upgrades to come.

On March 27, 2019, Karry hosted his final surprise for me, a 60th birthday party with family. As we concluded the event and exited the venue, there was his gift in the parking lot, adorned with a huge red bow. He was thrilled that I was happy.

While laying at the side of my husband, I remembered our special date and said, "Honey, you're leaving me before our thirty-fourth anniversary."

His response was, "Girl, you'd better count those weeks." We laughed as we continued our conversation.

He slept, and then around 3:00 a.m. he began another conversation by saying, "Baby, come take a walk with me." He verbally shared the sights he beheld in heaven and secrets I dare not utter. And then as I (along with Chris) eavesdropped on his conversation with Jesus, he said, "Jesus, that's *my* crown?"

I could only participate with my honey as a spectator that early morning, but one day I will be given the glorious opportunity to take a walk with him as a participant. I am so looking forward to reconnecting with him, seeing all that he saw, and worshipping our Lord throughout eternity!

We will be together again.

11

Letters

CHRIS WESLEY

M<small>Y DAD WAS A</small> brilliant orator, but many who have read his published works would argue that he was a better writer than preacher. I'm not sure if he would have said that about himself, but I do know beyond a shadow of a doubt that he was far more comfortable writing than he was having conversations. Maybe it was because of his introverted nature or his preference to avoid engaging in conflict. Whenever Dad had a real issue, he didn't call you to the office or initiate a verbal conversation. When Dad really wanted to communicate with you in a way that you could understand, he wrote a letter.

Over the course of my life, Dad and I had lots of letter exchanges. He wrote letters when he was proud of me. I wrote letters to express my gratitude. He wrote letters when he was disappointed in me. I wrote letters to express my apology. He wrote letters about his future plans and ideas. I wrote him letters about the things God was putting in my heart. I won't get any more letters from Dad, but here is one last letter to him:

Dad,

If there's one thing I've always been convinced of, I know that I am your pride and joy. My earliest memories are running to sit with you in the pulpit when you finished preaching when I was a toddler and how excited you were to let me come. I remember always wanting to ride with you to your preaching engagements around the city and how happy you were that I wanted to be with you. I remember how you responded when I gave my life to Jesus at the tender age of four. When I walked the aisle, you gave me the microphone and had me recite John 3:16 and Romans 10:9 to show the church that I knew the decision I was making. I remember how happy you were on the Sunday you baptized me. Your smile during my childhood is etched in my heart. As a child, I decided that I always wanted to make you smile.

Things started to shift a bit when I turned twelve. I made a lot of mistakes. I acted out a bit in school. I experimented with some things I shouldn't have. I struggled with my temper and found myself in some situations that I shouldn't have been in. I disappointed you at times, but we both knew that I was wrestling with the call God had on my life. I heard Him speak to me, and it scared me. I acted out to run away. You loved me too much to let me. You disciplined me and taught me the importance of heeding God's voice. During that season, you taught me that I did not want the consequences connected to disobedience. You knew what I was battling with because you had been there. You let God do His work in me.

I remember when I told you that God called

me to preach, like it was yesterday. Your response is etched in my heart. With a big smile you told me that you knew. You told me about how your dad called you a couple of days before and told you that God promised him that I would preach before God called him home. I remember how big you smiled as I preached that night as a nervous fifteen-year-old boy. You beamed with pride. One of my favorite pictures is from that moment. I'm your pride and joy.

I could recount a million moments like these. Moments like the Bishop 5 + 1 Revival in 2012 when we preached together; or on Father's Day in 2016 when you invited me to come preach at Antioch as a gift to you; or my first college touchdown. Despite all the moments I know I let you down and disappointed you, more than anything, I remember that you were proud of me.

Over the last couple months, I would like to think that you have been proud of me. I hope you were proud when I honored your wishes and preached your eulogy. I hope you were proud as I did my best to stand in your stead in the weeks after you got your crown. I hope you were proud as Antioch overwhelmingly voted for me to be your successor. For the rest of my life, I will do my best to make you proud. Hopefully, I can make you proud as a partner. One day, I hope to make you proud as a parent. I hope to make you proud as a pastor.

I haven't always been a perfect son, but I realize that your pride in me isn't rooted in perfection. You are proud of me because I am yours. As I'm writing this, I guess I am realizing what you have always wanted me to know. I don't have to do anything to make you proud of me. You always have been. You always will be. Thank you for your example. Thank you for your mantle. Thank you for the lessons. I'm honored to be your legacy.

Your eldest,
Chris

12

He Never Left Me

KARL C. WESLEY

I REMEMBER BEING A young kid in the summertime visiting my grandfather in Camden, Arkansas. Pops would wake me up at 4:00 or 5:00 a.m.

"Wake up, son. You going fishing with me?"

I'd pop up immediately. "Yes sir!"

I would get ready so fast. I loved going to his secret fishing spots to kick back and fish all day. We would go with our reels, bait, and chairs ready and with plenty of sandwiches so we wouldn't have to go anywhere. We could just relax! There wouldn't be much talking. I remember once asking him why we had to be so quiet. Back then, he told me the main reason was so we wouldn't scare the fish. But as I grew older, I knew another reason was because this was one of his avenues to get away and reflect.

My dad was an intellectual thinker, a human processor. He would literally take the information he received and break it all down before he even responded. If he had nothing to say to you, it was because he was still thinking it through. That's one of the reasons I knew that every word that came out of his mouth was real: they were calculated. It's funny because yes, Pops was a phenomenal speaker, literally one of the best and most articulate human beings to walk this earth (especially in a public arena), but my, he was not a talkative person. I can honestly say that Pops probably wrote or typed more words than he spoke over his life.

His writings—his speeches, his sermons, his books, his poems—man, his pen game was so eloquent and refined, yet still so transparent and real. Anything my dad ever wrote, you can literally read it and feel him through the page. That is great when you are reading one of his books or something, but when you are reading a two- or three-page letter that's written to Chris, Karl, or Charles— listen, it's one of the most gut-twisting experiences you'll ever have.

So look, my brothers and I have given our Pops plenty of head- aches over the years. I mean, we are all versions of him, and he couldn't stop some of it. But when we would get into trouble as teens, Pops wouldn't react immediately. Like I said before, he's a human processor. He would let us know that it would be dealt with later.

At this point, you'd wish he would just "swing on you," because now you know he is about to break it down and how hard he's really about to go! Next thing you know, you would come home, and a letter would either be waiting for you on your bed, or he would literally hand it to you, as if he was serving a warrant or something. He would tell you to read it with comprehension, and then he'd say, "We'll sit down later."

These letters would give you a complete analysis of what was done wrong, why you knew better in the first place, things you probably didn't even know he knew about, the options of what would happen going forward (which as a kid were horrible options, might I add), and just everything you didn't want to hear—in letter form.

Then we would sit down and talk; those were the toughest dis- cussions—looking him in the eye and knowing how disappointed he was in certain actions, and him reminding you of everything he's shown you by example and taught by his movements. I'm telling you that after a while, Pops didn't even have to put hands on us. His looks could pinch your soul when he was mad. But one thing I noticed was that he never lost his cool. Trust me, I gave him *plenty* of reasons to go crazy on me. But no matter the punishment, no matter the initial strain my actions might have caused over the years, he made sure to always show me he would be there to push me to be who he knew I was destined to be.

When I was young, running around the city with my boys trying to earn street credit by any means necessary, Pops *not once* told me that I needed to stop hanging with those guys. He didn't consider them bad influences because he knew that I knew better. I was supposed to be the "light" anywhere I went, so peer pressure wasn't an excuse. He held all of us accountable, and he also knew that everybody's path to the highest version of themselves is not the same.

As a close, I remember sitting down with Pops when I was in between jobs a couple years back. At this point, we both knew that I was done with nine-to-five jobs. I was itching to work in my passions, videography and photography, in some capacity. I refused to give my time to anyone else's dream other than my own. I knew at this point that he was just waiting for me to ask him for a job, and he was right. When I finally got up the nerve, we sat down, negotiated the terms, and then he initially told me I would be working with Facilities, which was fine with me! When it was time for me to start my first day, I was informed that he had switched some things up so I could become the new on-staff photographer at the church. He knew where my heart, talent, and passion were, and he acted on it. I was too happy. It meant a lot to me that he would make room for my gift.

After his passing, I realized that I, his son, had been taking what would be the visual chronicles for the last two years of his life. I'm so grateful that, in retrospect, I see how God set it up that way long before I even stopped working in corporate America.

Not only was I with him every Sunday and stopping by after

work, but the last month of his life I was with him every day. Back in the beginning of October 2019, I witnessed for the first time my dad having a "breathing attack" caused by all the cancer that had taken over his body. I told my mom right then that I would be there every day to help with whatever he or she needed. I have never been the one to handle anyone close to me being in pain; it hurts me to the core. So seeing my father, my superhero, hurt without rest tore me apart. I had to witness my dad's everyday struggle to live. But one thing I noticed is how happy my dad was that I was there.

Being men, we don't want our significant others to have to carry our burdens. Dad felt so bad for my mom. He apologized every day that he was putting her through that. But then I realized that's what he had sons for, to carry that extra weight when it was time. That's what my brothers and I did until the end.

Pops taught me so much about life. He was the epitome of a godly man on this earth. The way he fought until the very end, and what he stood for, will forever stick with me and push me until my time is over. His body isn't here, but he never left me.

Love you, Man,

Karl

13

Baby Boy

CHARLES WESLEY

THIS IS THE FIRST time since my father's death that I've put our relationship into words; and to be honest, it is impossible for me to express all that my father was for me. Although still grieving, I am at peace reminiscing on the memories I got to share with my pop. Daily I'm reminded that who he was is instilled in me, and that starts with the fear of God. His support, humor, and loyalty are just a few characteristics that my dad displayed within our relationship. His discipline, passion, and wisdom were displayed for the world.

I remember being young and asking Pops, "How do you battle complacency? How do you fight through the times you may not want to do the work?"

He took a breath, and in his calm voice he said, "Nah, that's not how I view it." He simply stated, "When you're supposed to do something, you do it because you're supposed to." Nothing deep, and it never was with my pop. He knew his purpose. This statement just reflects the way he lived his life.

For a moment, I want to reflect on our early relationship, the true role model he was, and the last chapter of his life that I was able to be a part of.

By the time I came around, my parents had the whole "boy thing" down pat. Being the baby was simple; I got the coolest versions of who my parents were. There would be times growing up that he would be mad at Chris and Karl about things and come talk to me about it. He was not looking for me to give feedback, but he for sure wanted a couple of "I understand" replies in there. As I got older, our relationship continued to strengthen, and he wanted that. Through the ups and downs, my pop was never afraid to use himself as an example, even for the bad times. He never wanted us to think he was perfect.

I played basketball throughout high school and two years in college at Henderson State University. My father would show up to every single game, even if he didn't tell my mom he was coming. He would be in the top row, cheering me on win or lose. It brought him joy watching me compete in something he personally had no interest in doing. He loved it so much just to be there, and knowing that I was the last son, he took every single advantage to come see me play.

For my two years at Henderson State, we talked on the phone very often. He was somebody I leaned on as a friend. We talked about everything, whether it was basketball, class, life, or a new set of cousins I just met that said we were family. I think of these days as the peak of our relationship. There was just no filter, and Pops enjoyed talking through these times with me.

I've always been appreciative and grateful for having my dad, but it took me seeing others to know how rare of a man he was. Everything wasn't perfect, but that is where my role model was the strongest. He was here. I never had to wonder where he went because he was here. Home. With his wife and kids. He didn't leave when it got "hot." He was a proud provider. His obligation as a pastor was second to his obligation as a father. Taking care of my mom and brothers genuinely made him happier than anything in the world. His loyalty toward us outlasted his love for us. No matter what we needed, he was there. No matter what time, he was there. The bad part about it was, you may not even want to need him, knowing the mood he would be in coming to save you. His calmness through times of turmoil was admirable. He never looked rushed or influenced. His wisdom always seemed to rise above the situation. He wasn't emotionally driven when it came to decisions he made. He simply leaned on God's voice for everything. Early on, I didn't understand, but as I got older, I noticed the key to his life was listening to God. My role model feared God.

This last part vaguely describes the last chapter of his life from my perspective. Simply, my father and I had been through a lot, not seeing eye-to-eye in multiple things, even to the point of not talking to each other. It hurt us both, but that's when the stubbornness we both had looked at each other in equal measures. It just felt like I didn't have my best friend for a long time. I made a lot of mistakes that cut my father deeply, to the point I was scared for our relationship. I just wanted to prove myself right so that one day my dad would possibly be impressed, that one day he could look at me and realize it all worked out for the better. Eventually, that was the least of my concerns.

I traveled back from Los Angeles in May 2018, after having been gone for seven months. Before I got off my flight, I remember jokingly asking myself, *Why did I come back again?* But being gone for so long, I wanted to see my mom, whom I consistently communicated with. I came back without warning. My parents, including my dad, were surprised and happy to see me. I sat in the computer chair as he came through the garage door, and in a kind of surprised voice he said, "What's up, Son?" I dapped him up and gave him a hug. I was happy. I was so happy. Just knowing how much we had to work to get our relationship back to good, I was so happy. This moment that was so small was so huge for me. He was proud of me. He was happy to see me. He embraced me. It felt as if everything we went through was all in the past.

That day sits with me more than any. My father forgave me. I just wanted him to see that I had matured, both spiritually and mentally. I wanted to show him that I had learned from the work ethic and passion he always displayed for me. I wanted to show him that I could be disciplined enough to take care of myself as a man and be mindful of the decisions I made on a day-to-day basis. I was happy to be back home, but soon we got the news that changed everything.

A couple of weeks later, we got the news that Dad had stomach cancer. Obviously, we were all devastated. We sat as a family having a detailed discussion, but the main focus of this conversation wasn't the sickness. Our father was challenging my brothers and me to make specific changes he wanted to see. That's my dad. He was always looking for light in dark times. In his mind, the lows in life were only to be used to show how far God can bring you. He walked that.

I could tell that my father was worried, but he never lost faith. Even knowing the seriousness of the disease, he still tried to disguise his pain from us, as any superhero would. He fought that disease and never lost. He beat it. And the biggest blessing was that our relationship never changed, even when he thought he was cancer-free. I was able to be here for my father through this time, and this meant the entire world to all of us.

Looking back on it, the cancer was minimal. I thank God for the grace He permitted throughout this last chapter. It was a true honor being the youngest son in this family.

A couple of weeks before he died, I asked my father if he had seen the changes from me that he wanted to see the day he informed us of the cancer. He swiftly said yes. The same cool relationship we came in with was the same he went out with. I'm forever grateful.

He said "good-bye" to us in order of our birth, and just as cool as ever, he looked and said, "Baby Boy, you're going to be all right," as he dapped me up. To the best father, the best husband, and the best papa, I simply say thank you for the light you shed on this world and household. Your legacy will continue to shine. We will continue to celebrate the life you lived.

Peace,

"Baby Boy" Charles Wesley

SECTION III

New Family Ties

14

Lasting Memories
of Karry Don Wesley

WILLIE AND ANGELA SMITH

The Early Years: A Fraternity Brother First

I DON'T RECALL MEETING Karry formally, but I do recall knowing of him a few years before becoming his brother-in-law in 1985. We shared a common bond forged by being initiated as brothers into the same fraternity, Alpha Phi Alpha Fraternity, Inc. I was initiated in 1983 at North Texas State University, while Karry had been initiated a few years earlier at Bishop College.

I can remember attending regional and national conventions in the early 80s. It was at one of these events at an oratorical competition that I heard Karry deliver Martin Luther King Jr.'s "I Have a Dream" speech. I was amazed by his recall and delivery of that speech. He recited the entire speech from memory—every single word of it! Unknowingly (at least to him) at that time, he had become one of my role models. He was my big brother in more ways than one.

KARRY AND CHERYL MARRY

I had always looked up to my big sister. Even as the youngest of three and the only boy of the family, I was very protective of both her and Carmelia. So when it came time for Cheryl and Karry to wed, I remember feeling at ease, comforted by the fact that my soon-to-be brother-in-law would take care of her. And Karry did not let me down.

OUR WEDDING DAY

When it came time to say "I do" to my bride-to-be in 1987, it seemed only appropriate to ask my brother and pastor, Karry, to perform our wedding ceremony. He agreed, and plans were made to marry Angela in the Carr P. Collins Chapel on the campus of Bishop College. But an interesting thing happened on our way to the altar. On the day of our wedding, the chapel flooded. As one would imagine, panic set in. Like some superhero, Karry went to work.

To this day I'm not sure how he pulled it off logistically, but he found us a church the day of the wedding. The word got out to our guests that the venue had changed, and we were married that same day as planned. What Karry did for Angela and me that day speaks to his willingness to step in and help at a moment's notice.

AS A FISHERMAN

Karry enjoyed spending time fishing. It seemed to offer the kid from Camden a measure of peace and tranquility away from the hustle and bustle of the city. Fishing was relaxing to him, and he was very good at it.

I was often amazed at how often he would catch fish—seemingly every time he went out. Without exaggeration, he'd always come back with a cooler full of fish. As if he'd perfected the science to it, Karry knew how to fish, when to fish, and where to fish.

On one occasion when the men of Antioch went out on an

annual fishing outing, I went along. I remember it being a hot day. I remember sweating in the heat for three or four hours fishing unsuccessfully. I decided, *Okay, this ain't working*, so I packed up. I walked along the bank and noticed a shaded, lightly wooded area. I then noticed Karry. He was alone. My brother had a nice setup. He had a stool or bucket of some sort to sit on, with a couple of rods baited in the water. The water appeared to be shallow with little to no movement. So I figured, *No way there's fish over here.*

I said, "Karry, man, what are you doing over here?"

He chuckled (probably because he could see that I was drenched in sweat). Without answering, he simply pulled his basket out of the water. In it were about ten to twelve fish that he'd caught.

RANDOM THOUGHTS AND OBSERVATIONS

Karry was a gifted man of God! His sermons would often have me asking, "How did he pull that out of that Scripture?!"

Karry was considerate, allowing me to drive his much larger car home from the hospital with my wife and our firstborn son when all we had at the time was a much smaller sports car.

Karry liked football and would show his support for his home team, the Dallas Cowboys.

All our kids (Alec, Michael, Evan, and Sydney) respected and cherished their Uncle Karry.

I will forever cherish the memories that I have of my beloved brother. I still miss you! I thank God that He brought you into our lives. Rest in perfect peace.

15

Like a Son

WILLIE E. SMITH SR.

ONE MORNING IN JUNE 1985, Karry came by the house and asked for permission to marry my daughter, Cheryl. I remember sitting down and asking him, "What did you say?" He repeated it. I then asked him one question: "Do you want as many kids as your parents had?" He told me no, which made me really happy! We talked about a few other things, and I gave him my permission and my blessing. Six months later, they were married. From that day on, he wasn't a son-in-law; he was like a son.

We would talk often, go fishing, and do lots of things together. I could never beat him fishing. When I did end up with a lot of fish, it was because he gave them to me. Many times I'd come home from work to find a cooler by my front door, full of catfish and crappie from Karry. He was some kind of fisherman!

He loved to work in his garden, too, growing cucumbers, tomatoes, greens, all kinds of peppers, okra, and squash. I always got whatever I wanted, especially the squash and okra because he really didn't like them.

If I asked him to do anything, he would do it with a smile. He was a great, great son. I remember him buying me a couple of

Dobbs dress hats several years ago, one brown and one black. I've been wearing them ever since. When they're not on my head, I place them in the boxes he gave me for storing them.

He was a good husband to my daughter; that's all I could ask for.

On his deathbed, he asked me, "Have I been a good son-in-law, Pop?"

I answered without hesitation, "You were the greatest!"

I really, really miss him and will miss him forever.

16

A Lifetime of Memories

TIA NICOLE

Life has always been a winding and unknown road, but Uncle Karry was always a giant light post that I could use as a guide home if my way got too far off track.

Knowing and loving Uncle Karry was a great experience. He was kind and gentle, always seeking ways to serve others. His giving spirit had no limits, yet he found time to love and cherish the ones closest to him.

Being loved by Uncle Karry was a special gift that only God could give. From a very young age, I was taught by Uncle Karry to not only love myself, but to love others first. He wanted me to believe that I could do anything I put my mind to as long as I kept God first. It took adulthood for me to understand the selfless lessons he drilled continuously through his "Unc Faith Lessons." He desperately wanted me to love God in a way that would fuel a lifetime of love and service in the presence of our almighty Savior.

Uncle Karry taught me that it was important to work and serve "as unto the Lord," even when it was the last thing I wanted to hear. I'm thankful that God thought enough of me to bless me with him.

Although my uncle is gone, he will forever be in my heart. I can honestly say, "It is well with my soul." Life is still a winding and unknown road. And although Uncle Karry's body is no longer here, the lifetime of memories will be my light post until I meet him again. I'm sad that he's gone, but I'm thankful that he got his crown. I will love him forever.

Brother, Pastor, Papa

PATRICE RILEY

BEFORE HE BECAME MY beloved brother, pastor, papa, Karry Wesley was the teaching pastor whose church my mother, husband, and our three tiny daughters visited repeatedly as if we were members, but we never officially joined early on. My cousin Audrey Faye Hudson introduced our family to this "inspiring pastor" and the "feeling of family" church home.

My mother, Dorothy Brazley, joined immediately after hearing this amazing young pastor preach. My mother said, "Many can have the name 'Pastor,' but few have the gift of supplying souls with spiritual comfort and teachings that reach out and touch you individually while in a group."

One Sunday after about a year of our visiting Antioch Fellowship, this inspiring pastor "opened the doors of the church," as was done each Sunday. My girls and I watched as several people joyously walked the aisles toward the front of the church, toward the pulpit. Clapping and amens were lovingly bestowed upon them as they heeded the call to learn more about our Lord and Savior Jesus Christ, become part of the Antioch church family, rededicate their lives, and steer their family toward a life promised.

At one point, this sharp pastor asked everyone to close their eyes and bow their heads. Pastor said, "I know there are more here, but you are too shy or waiting on someone to join church with you. There is also someone here—I do not know who or where you are—but you have little ones. They need a church home. They need to know more about their Savior. You are bringing them to the right place, but you need to go one step further. Raise your hand if that's you. Heads are down, eyes are closed."

I raised my hand, and then Pastor said the unthinkable: "Come on down. We are waiting for you. Bring your family."

My insides screamed *No!* I put my hand down quickly.

We did not join that Sunday, but did soon afterward, and we have been members for more than twenty-five years. I'm happy we joined! Our families grew closer, and our children Jasmine and Karl married years later. So many conversations and laughs were shared surrounding them and our three special gifts: Kamden, Karter, and Kyrin.

You will forever be my brother, pastor, papa.

18

My Hero for Life

JAMES RILEY

O NE SUNDAY MY WIFE came to me and said, "Pastor Wesley was looking for you at church today. He had a look on his face as if he had something important to tell you."

When I found out that he had cancer, my heart sank. Yet I was impressed with Pastor Wesley at how strong and transparent he was as he divulged his cancer diagnosis.

That day he was no longer just my pastor. He became my hero for life.

SECTION IV

We Called Him Friend

19

Remembering My Friend

PASTOR FELDER U. HOWARD

In the Word of God, Psalm 30:5 (KJV) assures us, "Weeping may endure for a night, but joy cometh in the morning."

I am reminded of the last communication that I received from Pastor Wesley, in the form of a letter. He closed it with "We will talk soon." Before we could talk again, the heavenly call to "Come up hither" came first, and my friend went home to be with our Lord Jesus Christ. Nevertheless, I still anxiously anticipate that moment when Karry and I will fellowship, talk, and rejoice again.

I had the privilege and blessed opportunity to meet him for the first time on a Wednesday night, in a fellowship service of the City-wide Brotherhood of Dallas, where I delivered the gospel message. I say that it was a blessed opportunity because I met a man who loved our Lord Jesus Christ with his whole heart. At that time in his life, there was no doctorate degree and no Antioch Fellowship Baptist Church; there was just a man called into the service of our Lord—sincere, dedicated, and humble. From that night on, we remained and still remain friends and brothers in our Lord.

I can vividly remember his first invitation for me to preach Antioch's first church anniversary service in the chapel of Bishop

College. It was a great day of worship and fellowship, all to the glory of God. Pastor Wesley's life is a testimony to the validity of Scripture. Matthew 6:33 (KJV) tells us, "But seek ye first the kingdom of God, and his righteousness; and all these things shall be added unto you." God continually added unto His dedicated servant both spiritually and physically. I was blessed to watch as God created a gospel preacher of great stature. I watched the faithfulness and dedication of his lovely wife to Christ, him, their family, and the church. I remember the Sunday afternoon when I first saw and held their firstborn son, a beautiful, fat, healthy baby boy, blessed of the Lord. And I rejoiced as Antioch Fellowship Baptist Church grew to be a beacon of light, to the glory of God, in the city of Dallas.

Yes, I miss my friend and brother, but I live with the knowledge that this mundane life that we now live is only temporary, a life where we are often required to experience the "night of separation." The Word of God tells us that the night of separation is only temporary. The night of separation will come to an end. "Weeping may endure for a night, but joy cometh in the morning." In the morning, in the presence of our Lord.

By faith I know that Karry Wesley and I will talk and rejoice together again—soon! We will talk as we experience that eternal morning, in the abundance of eternal life, in the presence of the One who died that we might live. In the majestic and glorified presence of Jesus Christ, our living Lord, we will talk again—soon!

20

A Friend Indeed

REV. DR. WANDA BOLTON-DAVIS

WHEN I THINK OF Pastor Karry D. Wesley, two words come to mind: serious and excellence. I experienced Pastor Wesley to be friendly and cordial, but he was also solemn and a no-nonsense individual. He was an intellectual at heart and took scholarship very seriously. He executed ministry with excellence. To visit the Antioch Fellowship Missionary Baptist Church was to experience excellence in every facet of ministry: from hospitality, to ministry staff, structure, and strategy, to the immaculate edifice itself. When it came to Pastor Wesley's preaching, he was masterfully skillful at alliteration and illustrations. His sermons were always incredibly memorable and transportable. I always walked away with his points and stories creatively etched into my heart.

The first time I met Karry Wesley was in 1980 on the notable campus of Bishop College, in Dallas, Texas. I had come to Bishop College with my friend Denny and his parents to begin Denny's freshman year. After a long thirteen-hour tiring drive from Illinois, we arrived on Bishop campus only to learn that there was "no room in the inn." Denny did not have a dorm room assignment. We were all shocked with disbelief. Bewildered and perplexed, we began to brainstorm for solutions. It seemed as if there was nothing else to do but for us to turn around and begin the taxing journey back to Illinois. However, when it seemed as though all hope was lost, an upperclassman, Karry Don Wesley, said he was willing to take in a roommate. I can remember the elation and relief that we all felt at Karry's invitation. In just a few hours, we got Denny unpacked, said our goodbyes, and headed back to Illinois.

Little did I know that three years later, in 1983, I would marry that young man, Denny, and relocate to Dallas. In 1985, Karry married Cheryl. It wasn't long until Cheryl and I became dear friends. In those early years as young couples, we were busy with the responsibilities of ministry, working, having babies, raising children, and supporting our husbands in ministry. Throughout the years, I heard the "roommate story" rehearsed over and over. It was not only a reminder of Karry's compassion and longtime friendship, but also of God's gracious provision in the time of need.

Over the years, both our ministries grew, and so did our friendship. Cheryl and I talked together, walked together (literally, we exercised), cried together, and shared many stories. Though my interaction was mainly with Cheryl, Karry was my brother. I always had deep respect for him. In 2004, when I published my first book, *Victorious Disciples*, Karry wholeheartedly granted my request to write an endorsement.

A few years later, although I had been speaking for many years, I wasn't certain how the acknowledgment of my call into the gospel preaching ministry would impact my relationship with Karry. Anyone who knew him knew his stance on women in ministry. However, to my surprise, despite our theological differences, he invited me to speak for the women of Antioch on several occasions. Needless to say, we had an unspoken understanding. He knew he could trust me to exercise my spiritual gift, while at the same time respect his leadership and the order of the house.

When my marriage of thirty-five years went through an unimaginable storm, Karry was one of only a few pastors who reached out with words of encouragement and support. He said, "Sis, I'm praying for both of you. I'm praying you will work it out." He went on to say, "You are always welcome to the Antioch Church," and then he tagged it with "and feel free to bring your books."

As I write with tearing eyes, that phone call meant the world to me. I will forever remember his thoughtfulness. Not only did it demonstrate what type of friend Karry Wesley was, but it exemplified the great man, the caring pastor, and the true Christian he was.

Pastor Karry Don Wesley, may your sermons continue to preach! May your illustrations continue to inspire! May your friendship continue to encourage! May your legacy continue to live!

"A friend loves at all times, and a brother is born for a time of adversity" (Proverbs 17:17 NIV).

21

Homeboys

PASTOR TERRY WHITE

I MET KARRY WHEN I came to Dallas to pastor the Mount Carmel Baptist Church in 1988. Although I did not matriculate at Bishop College, I was privileged to become close to some of the Bishop Five through Pastors Denny Davis, Jeffery Johnson, and Anthony Sharp, along with Willis Johnson, who coordinated this effort to support Paul Quinn College on the campus of the defunct Bishop College.

It was through my relationship with Karry that I was inspired to attend Brite Divinity School on the campus of Texas Christian University in Fort Worth.

Karry and I discovered that we both were from the only state in the nation that's in the Bible, Arkansas—Noah looked out of the ark and saw! I am from Stamps, Arkansas, the setting of the late renowned poet Maya Angelou's autobiography, *I Know Why the Caged Bird Sings*. Karry was from Camden and knew and went to school with my relatives. I would often talk about our upbringing in our native state.

I have several wonderful memories that he and I shared. I remember getting called to pastor the Marsalis Avenue Baptist

Church in 1998. Karry would always honor me by inviting me to preach at Antioch Fellowship on several occasions. I was honored because he treated me as though I pastored a large church congregation, and that made me feel so proud and inspired.

My love and appreciation for Karry grew, and our friendship blossomed. We didn't talk on a daily basis, but whenever we needed each other, we would be there for one another. He was a pastor with a great heart in giving to other pastors.

I always looked up to Karry and admired how he did ministry. We developed a close relationship when my son, who is now a medical surgeon, attended the summer camp at Antioch Fellowship. He made a significant impression on him as well.

I would often share with Karry how impressive it was that he allowed the Holy Spirit to grow and develop the church spiritually and numerically, and never removed Missionary Baptist from the church's name. That was a highlight for me to watch how gracefully he did ministry. He really inspired me with all the accomplishments and achievements he attained in such a short life.

22

Kinship

PASTOR O. C. COLLINS

WE ALWAYS USE THE expression that there are people we "look up to." To me, it means that there are certain individuals who have left a lasting impression or blazed a trail or served as a role model. That being said, I could easily place Karry Wesley in all those categories. However, Karry Wesley had such an impact on my life that he transcends being one to look up to.

I first became aware of his caring heart when he came to the homegoing service for my father. I had never met him, but believed I knew him because my brother Tim talked about him so highly. After meeting him, our friendship, or should I say "kinship," was automatic.

Next I became aware of his intense love for his family and church. He approached both as duty and obligation. This strengthened our bond, and we spent hours exchanging experiences (good and bad), as well as ideas and strategies. I cannot adequately share all that I would like to in any amount of words; there are just not enough.

Most of the places here in Memphis that Karry and I used to frequent during his visits have changed or are no longer in business;

however, the memories that I have with my brother will always occupy the locations.

He was a prolific writer, accomplished teacher, dynamic preacher, excellent pastor, dedicated family man, and my friend. All these things make Karry Wesley not a man for me to look up to, but a man to "live up to."

Encourager

PASTOR BRYAN CARTER

A S A YOUNG PREACHER and pastor, you don't know what you don't know. One of my early efforts was to try to meet with some local pastors in our community for counsel and advice. I called and attempted to schedule time with a few of them. Pastor Wesley took my meeting request, and he was incredibly gracious to me.

We met in the old church location on Hampton, and when I walked in I saw a few books that he had written, including one on the book of James. I was so impressed and immediately asked him about the books. He shared his heart for not just preaching and teaching, but also for providing resources for the body of Christ. This struck a chord with me because not many pastors have the gifts and vision that Pastor Wesley had. His writing ministry would continue to flourish to include ten books.

We sat down and talked that day, and I brought a series of questions which included: How did he prepare his sermons? What advice did he have for a young pastor? How do you lead through change? What mistakes should I avoid? How do you preach a sermon series? How do you manage being in school and pastoring?

How can I balance family and ministry? How do you lead a staff? I had lots of questions. We spent about an hour in conversation, and I gained so much from that time together.

That meeting would be the beginning of many more conversations over the course of the next sixteen years. I needed lots of help, and Pastor Wesley was generous enough to offer counsel, advice, wisdom, resources, and prayer. I learned so much just watching him lead and watching him guide his church. He was a visionary and an exceptional pastor who not only could articulate a clear vision, but he had the administrative gifts to execute those plans. I remember when the current Antioch campus was just a vision. I watched him as he led through every phase and transition—this showed me what leadership looked like.

Early in our relationship, he was the first in the city to invite our church to do a church exchange. We went to Antioch, and he brought Antioch to Concord. We normally did it in the Thanksgiving season, and it was a great highlight for me. As a young preacher, I enjoyed fellowshipping with Antioch and learning so much from how he led and pastored his church. This fellowship allowed our churches to build relationships, and it was an incredible joy for my wife and I to be in presence of the Wesleys and spend time with them. I always left encouraged.

Pastor Wesley's passion for family was always something I admired. Many times when I would see him in the city, he was talking about his sons, their sports, and following his sons around the city and state to support and cheer them on. The Wesleys had a deep appreciation for family, and it was always encouraging to me. When the church built his office, he had a space for his family, which I thought was a genius idea. Pastor's children spend a lot of time at church, and it was great idea to have family space. When we built our church, we did the same thing, and it has helped us keep family a priority, which Pastor Wesley modeled so well.

I remember when Pastor Wesley led Antioch to address the injustice of the termination of former City of Dallas Police Chief

Terrell Bolton. This injustice was a tremendous issue in our community and caused great concern for the Dallas community. Scriptures consistently call people of faith to be engaged in pursuing matters of righteousness and justice. Pastor Wesley led them to take buses of members to meetings and protests to address this grave injustice. They wore T-shirts and advocated and stood for justice in this important case. He taught me in this moment how to be civic-minded and engaged as a pastor.

I recall Pastor Wesley's great love for the Word of God. Second Timothy 2:15 (kjv) states, "Study to shew thyself approved unto God, a workman that needeth not to be ashamed, rightly dividing the word of truth." Pastor Wesley took this verse seriously, and he invested much in being well prepared when he stood to declare God's Word. Whether I was watching him online, on TV, or in person, Pastor Wesley consistently handled the Scriptures with integrity and intentionality. I've stolen—I mean "borrowed"—a number of his great illustrations that I've loved because he had a knack for communicating so clearly. He was a model for many in terms of biblical preaching.

Pastor Wesley was generous. He was always willing to share his resources and the resources of Antioch to help build up the body of Christ. He had a kingdom mindset focused not just on building Antioch, but also on building the kingdom of God. For a number of years, when the L. K. Williams Ministers Institute needed a location and revitalization, he stepped up in a major way. This institute was an annual historic gathering for preachers to learn and grow in preaching and ministry from the days of Bishop College. When Dean Rollins of Bishop College needed a partner, Pastor Wesley was quick to support and resource the conference. This conference was an annual highlight for me to hear great preachers and to learn tools for ministry for myself and our team. When Antioch celebrated their twenty-fifth church anniversary, Pastor Wesley invited different Dallas pastors and churches for worship services. I believe he invited more than forty churches during the course of that year, and it spoke volumes for building relationships and building the body of Christ in Dallas.

Finally, Pastor Wesley was extremely supportive. The Scriptures celebrate the relationship that Paul had for Timothy and how Paul invested in Timothy, encouraged Timothy, and helped Timothy to understand ministry and live out the Christian life. Pastor Wesley found great joy in doing this for others. Throughout my ministry, he was a constant source of encouragement. He was a genuine cheerleader for me. When I celebrated my tenth pastoral anniversary, he was so excited for me. I wasn't alone, for there are many members and ministers who were recipients of the love and support of Pastor Wesley. Pastor Wesley was generous in sharing his love and support for others.

I still think of him often, and the memories of life will linger with us for years and years to come. We have to be thankful for the memories and for what God did through his life. His life still seems so short, but I marvel at all that God did through him. I am reminded of the lyrics of that song, "May the Works I've Done Speak for Me": "When I'm resting in my grave, there's nothing more to be said."

The works of Pastor Karry Wesley definitely speak volumes about his love for God and his love for God's people, and we are forever grateful.

24

Iron Sharpens Iron

PASTOR OSCAR EPPS

T HE LOOMING QUESTION USUALLY is, "How did you and Dr. Wesley become such good friends?" We were both founding pastors who had experienced incredible moves of God. We were both married to phenomenal *über*-helpmates. We also shared an affinity for a good laugh! However, I truly believe God knitted our hearts together to encourage each other.

The wisdom of Proverbs reminds us that "iron sharpens iron." I can truly say that Karry Wesley sharpened me as a man.

Dr. Wesley sharpened me for ministry as well. I can vividly remember when our church had approximately two hundred members. Karry really didn't know me; however, I invited him to preach for our church's anniversary celebration, not overly optimistic that he would accept. He gladly responded by saying, "I will do whatever I can to assist you." We were extremely blessed by his inspiring message. I was so appreciative that although his church membership was approximately 4,500 strong, he didn't think it was a waste of time. After that moment, we began to form a strong bond of friendship. Karry gave me wisdom and advice that sustains me still today.

He also sharpened me with ministry exposure. I have been blessed to be a facilitator for the last few years at his annual men's conference. At the end of the conference the very first year, he gave me a 1099 form. I hadn't seen one before, so I asked, "What is this for?"

He just laughed and replied, "Oscar, this means you're going to make at least six hundred dollars."

The gentle giant saw in me what perhaps I didn't see in myself. He always pushed me to be better. I was also honored to preach his Twenty-fifth Silver Anniversary Celebration.

But then things changed. Once he was diagnosed with cancer, it was my turn to pour into him! The Lord led me to organize a benefit prayer service in his honor. He actually thought he could somehow talk me out of it. But I insisted! "Not only have you been a blessing to me, but you have helped countless others. A service to honor you will be done!"

In hindsight, I'm thankful that he was able to smell some of his proverbial flowers. Still, there was no way to encapsulate all the goodwill he had showered upon others.

Ultimately, we have bowed to God's sovereignty. I will forever miss my dear friend.

25

Our Pastor, Our Friend

CHARLES AND DR. J. HELEN PERKINS

THE PERKINS FAMILY—CHARLES, HELEN, Crystal, and Casey— were privileged to meet the Wesley family more than thirty years ago at Antioch Fellowship Missionary Baptist Church. The bond was instant because not only was Dr. Wesley our Pastor, but he was also our friend and brother, whom we dearly love. We shared many emotions together, such as joy, laughter, sorrow, and sadness, as we shared each other's stories and challenges. We have continued admiration, respect, and appreciation for our pastor and brother. He was a kind, honest, loyal, understanding, and sincere friend.

At church, Pastor would walk up to us and say, "Pray for me"; then he would walk away to prepare for his sermon. After he preached, he would return to our presence and thank us for the prayers; he felt God's support while he preached. We are sure that several of us were always praying for our pastor.

He saw so much more in Charles than we all knew or considered. Pastor called and requested that he serve as a speaker on Annual Men's Day. Charles did not feel qualified and believed that there were many men in our church who were qualified to speak. When Charles asked, "Why me?" Pastor said, "Why not you?"

When encouragement is needed, I remember the motivating words of my pastor, brother, and friend who supported me with confidence and assurance.

Pastor had another request that Charles become assistant youth director and work with the young males in the church; of course, the answer was yes. Your response to Pastor was yes.

He selected Charles to become a deacon; after a year of studying and learning what it meant to be a deacon, I became a deacon and eventually a trustee.

We studied a book written by Pastor Wesley; we learned so much from our pastor and teacher. Charles continues to serve as a leader in the church; he had a great teacher and mentor.

We grew into better followers of Christ as Pastor Wesley preached and taught us about God and how to build a better relationship with God. He was a master presenter of God's Word, but he would always encourage us to not just listen to him, but to study the Bible for ourselves. We have several notebooks of sermons that he preached, and we revisit those messages even today.

Pastor Wesley taught our daughters, Crystal and Casey, at a very young age, to take notes while he preached. They still take notes and they have taught their children to do the same. Once, Crystal looked at the program and wrote the title of the message, "Oh, What a Friend We Have in Jesus!"

Pastor stood and spoke the title of his message, "Oh, What a Friend We Have in Judas!"

Crystal looked at us and said, "That is not right," but then she looked in the program, and you know what the title was. He explained to us why Judas was our friend. Judas betrayed Jesus; Jesus went to the cross for you and me.

Cheryl and Pastor trusted us to babysit their boys, and the boys call us Aunt Helen and Uncle Perk!

We enjoyed babysitting the boys, even overnight while Pastor and Cheryl traveled out of state for a revival. They knew the boys were in a caring and loving environment; they were, and are, well loved by the Perkins family. At the ages of three, four, and beyond, Christopher would request that we get our Bibles and sit down while he preached to us. We were all four obedient. He would tell us, "Turn to John 3:16," and that was his message. Of course, he had that Scripture memorized! Chris baptized all the stuffed animals in our house, and he quoted the baptismal words that he heard his father say many times.

Our brother shared with us that once, when Karl was very young, he was on his knees praying, and he thanked God for his two dads! When Karl finished praying, Pastor asked him who his second dad was. Karl said, "Uncle Perk." This is such a special story, and we all laughed. Of course, Pastor pretended that he was concerned about Karl's second dad! There were several times that we shared stories such as these and laughed. Charles, the youngest Wesley son, has the same name as Charles; that is so special to us.

Pastor had such a passion for others. He was there when Helen's mother passed, providing our family the strength we needed. He came to the funeral and prayed with us as we struggled through a difficult time. He's our brother and stood alongside us during some of our most difficult times. Pastor was a follower of Christ, a servant of God as he served others.

Pastor and I shared the experience of becoming doctors in our chosen fields; we shared the challenges. We supported each other with talks and prayer as we traveled through the challenging journey of becoming doctors. We made it. God blessed both of us—Dr. Wesley in 1997 with his Doctorate of Ministry and Dr. Perkins in 1999 with a Doctorate in Instruction and Curriculum Leadership/Literacy. We both acknowledged that we grew through this demanding process.

When we moved to Memphis more than fifteen years ago, Pastor came a few times to preach revivals. Of course, we would attend those revivals, and he would ask us to stand. Then he would introduce us. He shared with the audience that the Perkins family was only on loan to Memphis; we were still his members. That introduction made us feel so loved and that he cared about our family. Our friendship remained for all those years, and we kept in touch even though we were miles apart.

When Helen experienced discrimination at a literacy conference, the experience became a part of Pastor's sermon since he, too, knew the pain of discrimination.

For more than thirty-one years, we did life together with the Wesleys. We enjoyed visiting each other. We would visit in the Wesley's home and enjoyed delicious food and fellowship. He blessed us with his wisdom that remains with us. Our pastor has changed his physical address as he now resides in heaven, but he will always be a part of our lives. His positive impact continues to be strong in the lives of the Perkins family, and we are grateful that God chose our paths to cross.

SECTION V

God's People at Antioch

26

My Brother, My Friend

REV. CARL SLEDGE SR.

But as it is written, Eye hath not seen, nor ear heard,
neither have entered into the heart of man, the things
which God hath prepared for them
that love him.
1 Corinthians 2:9 (KJV)

GOD LOVED KARRY, AND Karry loved the Lord. These things I know for certain. Karry loved the Lord, his wife, his sons, his family members, his friends, and others.

Karry Don Wesley—my brother, my friend. It all began with Cheryl Ann. Cheryl, Carmelia, and Willie Jr. loved and chose me to be their big brother. Mother Bettie and Willie Earl Sr. are godparents to my oldest son, Carl Jr. We all loved watching television together, along with other members of the youth department where my mother, Mary K. Ellison, served as youth director.

Cheryl and I enjoyed studying the Sunday school lesson for hours on the telephone.

While attending Bishop College, Karry would worship with us at Carver Heights Baptist Church. Karry and Cheryl started dating. Karry loved Cheryl, and early in their relationship Karry called me feeling a little down. He was unhappy with the fact that he was unable to do more for Cheryl. His finances didn't allow it.

Cheryl had a good job and a nice sports car. He said, "Man, Cheryl has to ride me around in her car."

I said, "If that doesn't bother her, don't let it bother you. One day you are going to buy Cheryl a car." I said, "As a man, I understand, but let it go."

We became close and our friendship grew. He would say to me, "Man, I love to hear you preach."

While Karry was still at Bishop, the Lord gave to me two dreams. In the first dream we were on a hospital elevator, going to minister to the sick. The Lord said, "Stay with him." The second dream was as the first, on an elevator. But this time he was wearing a tan London Fog all-weather coat. The Lord said, "Stay with him."

I asked the Lord, "What does the coat mean?"

The Lord said, "Jacob had twelve sons, but he made only one coat. I have chosen Karry; stay with him."

Time passed, and just as the Lord had revealed, we went to the hospital. Karry parked the car, went into the trunk, and pulled out a tan London Fog all-weather coat. The elevator scene in my dream became a reality.

After the visit, I told Karry my dreams during lunch. Neither one of us knew God's plan, but we knew God had a greater purpose for his life.

Karry asked me if I was okay with him marrying Cheryl. I gave him my blessings and was overwhelmed when he asked me to be his best man in their wedding.

One evening Karry stopped by my home, and in my driveway said, "Carl, I have access to Carr P. Collins Chapel on the campus of Bishop College. I want to gather the scattered members so we all can worship together in one place. I want you to go with me."

I said to him, "I've already promised the Lord that I would."

The two of us set out to do the Lord's will. God blessed us to go from scraping up money to rent the chapel one Sunday, to a beautiful edifice—"thirty-three and debt free!"

Because of his faithfulness and unwavering devotion, Karry found favor in the sight of the Lord. All of us have been blessed under his leadership.

During Antioch's early years, when Chris was young, he would often run to the pulpit and sit in his daddy's lap after Karry preached. Chris—only God knew that He was going to take you from your daddy's lap, call you, anoint you, and give you the power to preach His Word. Even at your father's funeral.

Karl—a few minutes after you were born, your Grandmother Bettie called me from the hospital and said, "Your namesake Karl is here, but it's spelled with a K instead of a C." We laughed. I was both humbled and happy that my brother thought enough of me to name one of his sons after me.

I loved him, and beyond a shadow of a doubt, I know that he loved me and my wife, Lena, as well. Before giving our wedding vows, he said, "Give me a minute." His eyes were teary, and he acted as if our marriage was an answer to his prayer.

In closing, my brother and my friend, chosen as a child, anointed and appointed by God, served the Lord with gladness, in sickness and in health. He has exchanged his shoes for golden slippers. He has exchanged his clothes for a long white robe. He has exchanged his cross for a crown, singing a song not even the angels can sing—redeemed, redeemed, my soul has been redeemed. I'm really going to miss you, my brother. Karry is saying to us, "Celebrate, be happy for me. I've moved to a new location."

I'm not saying goodbye. I'm saying I'll see you later.

Free at last.

27

Time Well Spent

FRED FITTS

I FIRST MET PASTOR Wesley in 1983. I had been invited to worship with Harold Lilly at Carver Heights Baptist Church, where Tyler Carter was pastor.

The Sunday morning I attended the service, Pastor Carter wasn't present, and a young minister stood and delivered an excellent sermon. After the service, Harold Lilly apologized for the senior pastor's absence. I told him there was no need to apologize as the sermon was great. I inquired about the young man's name, and was told that it was Karry Don Wesley.

Shortly thereafter, my family and I joined Carver Heights Baptist Church. I became an active member, and Pastor Carter eventually requested that I work as director of the Shepherd Boys Group. I accepted the request and started to meet weekly with a group of eight young men. The group started to grow, and Pastor Carter recognized I needed some help. He invited me to a meeting of just three, where he introduced me to my new assistant, Reverend Karry Don Wesley.

Young Wesley was friendly, humble, and unusually quiet for a young man, but totally in tune with communicating with others. For the first few meetings, he would just listen and only comment sparingly.

I remember walking into a meeting where I had a particular Bible verse marked in my Bible for discussion. I showed it to Wesley, only to discover he had done research on the same verse.

Consider the fact that we had not discussed this information previously nor in any prior meeting. In that moment, I got a chill. I looked at him and said, "One day you're going to be my pastor." He just looked at me, but had no response. He just chuckled. I knew at that point he was special to me for an unknown journey.

I felt totally comfortable with Wesley taking the lead in all meetings, and I started to listen to him communicate ideas and insight to these young men. He had the ability to hold their attention and excite. Even in his youth, he carried himself in such a manner that respect was a must.

Wesley could raise their curiosity to a point where some discussions would carry over to the following meeting a week later. I thought this was a unique quality considering the attention span of the group involved.

Occasionally, Wesley would drop by my office in the Wynnewood Shopping Center for talks ranging from Shepherd Boys to fishing. I learned that in Camden, Arkansas, he fished constantly. I took him fishing and learned very quickly that if I didn't bring my "A" game, he could and did punish my ego.

Wesley would sit fishing for hours and not utter a word. I began to understand that the time spent sitting and fishing included prayer time with God. It got to the point that I would move a good distance from him so there were no distractions.

He was country to his core. I remember returning to the area he was fishing one day to find him sitting on a stool. I noticed at least four snakes crawling within two feet of him. Looking closer, there was another lying between his feet. I yelled for him to move. Wesley responded by saying, "Don't yell, you'll scare the fish away. Besides, those are just water snakes; they won't bite."

There were visits when he would come sit and talk about his young home life. He would graphically explain how he hadn't always been as forthright as the man he had grown into. He was especially grateful that his parents never gave up on him. He stated that his mom probably had sores on her knees from praying for him.

Wesley cherished his opportunity to show his family that he could and would succeed with the help of the Lord. He shared with me that he joined the Alpha Phi Alpha Fraternity, Inc. because he knew the history of some of the members. He mentioned Dr. Martin Luther King Jr., Thurgood Marshall, and Andrew Young, among others. It struck me that the names he mentioned all had political ties. I told him that if he became a successful politician, I wanted to ride in his helicopter as payment for spending so much of my valuable time with him. We laughed.

As we all know, college students don't have much money. Karry Wesley was no exception. I understood this and always made certain that I offered a few dollars on his visits to my office. While in college, he and others were only receiving fifty dollars per sermon. Yet young men do have tremendous appetites. Sometimes Wesley would show up at my office with his crew. He brought with him Freddie Haynes, Denny Davis, and Jimmy Baldwin. They were all just young, energetic, charismatic ministers back then. The high point of their visits with me had one purpose. They all needed money for "a two piece and a pepper" from Church's Chicken. Looking back, it was a blessing for me to do just a little something in God's long-range plan.

I remember inquiring about an old injury on his arm. Wesley explained that he had an incident where a brown recluse spider had bitten him and left the obvious wound. He said that during his hospital stay, a group of people had visited him from Carver Heights Baptist Church, and he enjoyed the visit and attention. It wasn't until quite some time later that he confessed that one of those visitors really got his full, undivided attention—Cheryl Smith.

When Karry Wesley came to my office and informed me that he was going to marry Cheryl, we had a very long visit. We sat for at least an hour and talked about our responsibilities as husbands. I used the *Godfather* movie as one illustration. I told him that in the movie, the old don explained that men can't afford to make mistakes. If he were to have a home and lose it, he would be the one criticized, not the wife. Therefore, his obligation was to use his wisdom to protect and provide for his family. I explained that the Bible says that he who puts himself last is then first in the sight of God. Take care of your family before yourself, and God will do the rest. It's obvious that he took his vows and commitment to his family seriously. He had three sons. Each is different, but I do see a young Karry Don Wesley in each of them.

I remember a telling incident when I was trustee chairman as we worshiped at Bishop College. I was passing by him after a service and mentioned to him that we needed to purchase some toiletries. At that point, funds were tight. He paused, looked at me, and said, "Let me pray on that."

I got a little frustrated because that was a small item to pray over. I started to walk away, but turned and asked, "Can't we do anything around here without praying first?"

Wesley looked at me and calmly said softly, "No."

Not for one second did I truly ever imagine that the young humble man I was counseling would one day be my pastor. Never did I dream that Karry Don Wesley, my fishing partner, would lead a group of believers like Antioch Fellowship Missionary Baptist Church. But I did know that he was special.

28

Journey to Antioch

MARY SMITH BRADLEY

When I'm sleeping in my grave,
and there's nothing to be said,
May the work I've done speak for me.
—Sullivan Pugh

INTRODUCTION

THE TWO WEEKS PRIOR to Pastor's passing, I had been watching President Trump's impeachment hearing on CNN. Some of the witnesses testified to what they heard from others, which is considered secondhand information. Others presented information that they experienced or were part of. Today, I am giving firsthand information. I was there when the following events happened.

I first met Reverend Karry Wesley, Reverend Jimmy Baldwin, and other ministers while they were students at Bishop College. They would attend Carver Heights Baptist Church each Sunday in their dark suits, shirts, and ties.

FAST-FORWARD TO APRIL 1986

It was time for the annual spring revival, and Pastor Brady Blade had informed the deacons of the church that he was not coming to conduct the services. The deacons met and decided to have Reverend Karry Wesley conduct the revival. Karry called my late husband, Marcus Dunn, and asked him what he should do. He told him, "Preach the Word!" These were five of the greatest nights of revival we had experienced as Karry expounded on the Word.

LOST SHEEP

During the next three months, because of discontent and unrest, some of us started visiting other churches. Some joined another church or stayed at home on Sunday mornings, like I did, and kept my money in my pocket.

A CALL FROM KARRY

On a hot summer day in August, Reverend Wesley called ten people and asked them to meet him at the Zale Library on the Bishop College campus. Those ten people called others, and almost two hundred people showed up to meet with him. We decided to worship in the Carr P. Collins Chapel. The worship service that first Sunday was attended by more than the people who were present at the meeting. We worshiped together several more Sundays, and the body decided to organize.

A committee was selected with the late Brother Samuel Booker as chairperson. The members were Lorene Richie Pitts, Nat Brown, Odell Brown, Annie Nelson, and me. The committee was to do the research and talk with local pastors. We were charged with getting the criteria and the procedures needed and bring this information back to the church body. The body accepted the criteria, and we organized.

Several church names were presented, and Samuel Booker suggested the name Antioch Fellowship Missionary Baptist Church.

Next we needed a pastor. After some discussion, Samuel Booker suggested that Reverend Karry D. Wesley be given a chance. The vote was unanimous! The 540 members were so happy to be together. The late John Calloway, Fred Fitts, and others gathered fans so that we could be comfortable in the chapel, which had no working air conditioning.

MINISTERIAL SUPPORT

During our infancy, Reverend Carl Sledge Sr. stood by Pastor Wesley, as did several local pastors. They included Dr. C. A. W. Clark of the Good Street Baptist Church, Reverend Floyd Harris of the Mount Tabor Baptist Church, the Reverend Felder Howard of the Rising Star Baptist Church, and the Reverend Earnest Freeney of the Dixon Circle Baptist Church.

LOOKING FOR A HOME

After several months of worshiping at Bishop College, a committee was selected to find us a church home. The committee members were Marcus Dunn, Lorene Richie Pitts, Joe Plouche, and Pastor Karry Wesley.

A property located at 7408 South Hampton Road, a family life center owned by Hillcrest Baptist Church, would accommodate our needs. The banks, however, would not give us a loan because we had not been organized a full year and had no financial track record. After much prayer and consistent giving by the Antioch membership, Hillcrest Baptist Church decided to finance the loan of $650,000 themselves. It didn't take long before the loan was repaid in full.

GROWTH AT 7408

The membership grew so fast in our new church home that a committee was charged with looking for a larger facility a few short years later. The back wall of the sanctuary was extended for a balcony to be erected with additional seating. We started having two worship services on Sundays and eventually moved to three services with overflow seating set up in the choir room and hallways. In the meantime, because of Pastor's consistent teaching of supporting the church financially, the property at 7408 was paid off, and undeveloped land at 7550 South Hampton was purchased.

MOVING AGAIN

The building committee found two locations and presented them to the church body. One was the Hillcrest Baptist Church property off Camp Wisdom, where the Concord Church now occupies; the second was property on Westmoreland, where the Inspiring Body of Christ Church's school is currently located. After much discussion and looking at the age of both buildings, we decided to build at 7550. Sister Lee McKinney was vice president at the bank and was extremely instrumental in our securing the loan for the building.

Our financial secretaries kept accurate and documented records of our finances. Those persons included Odell Brown, Willie Kimble, Willie Keeton, Dennis Hawkins, Stephan Booker, and Drew Wilborn.

The first phase of the building process was the multipurpose center, nursery, offices, classrooms, and a dedicated space for a commercial kitchen to be added at a later date. Once this phase was complete, we would sell the property at 7408 and in time build the sanctuary where we worship today.

Persons who worked with Pastor during those foundational years included Trustee Chairmen Marcus Dunn, Fred Fitts, Herbert Moore, and Joe Dean; Deacon Chairmen Nat Brown and James Bailey; and attorneys Thelma Clardy and Sonya Hoskins.

SOMETHING SPECIAL

It was important to share this church history so you could see how God has used Karry Wesley. I know this information to be true because I served on the trustee board for fifteen years and was board secretary for ten of those years.

God not only loved Karry Wesley, but He put His hand on him for something special.

THE FAMILY MAN

Karry loved his wife, Cheryl, and displayed what Paul said to the church at Ephesus: "Husbands, love your wives as Christ loved the church and gave himself for it" (Ephesians 5:25 NCV). Karry realized that they were one flesh, and he treated her with great love and care. He emulated Christ's love in their marriage.

His three sons, Chris, Karl, and Charles, were loved by him. He talked about each of them with such pride that his chest expanded. And those grandchildren had Papa's heart! He loved his siblings, as well, and shared stories of their upbringing and accomplishments. He loved his family.

THE VISIONARY LEADER

Karry had management skills, and he set goals, planned, organized, and implemented his plans with fidelity. He was a good listener and risk taker. He was intelligent and smart. He had the wisdom to surround himself with the right people to accomplish his goals.

THE SCHOLAR

He was a lifelong learner. His bachelor's degree in theology was not enough for him. He went on to also earn a master's degree in divinity (MDiv) and a doctorate in ministry (DMin).

He wanted to be prepared to lead.

THE AUTHOR

Pastor Wesley had a unique way of penning words. He could paint a picture of clarity with words.

He is the author of ten books that are read all over the United States, and he has created many Bible study curricula since the church's inception.

THE PREACHER

He began preaching as a teenager. He was a proclaimer of the Word and believed that the Holy Bible was the inerrant Word of God. He was careful to draw out the exact meaning of a passage.

He preached the plan of salvation from Romans 10:9. He preached, "The wages of sin is death; but the gift of God is eternal life" (Romans 6:23 KJV).

He preached the gospel, the good news, and could preach to any audience.

PASTOR AND TEACHER

And he gave some, apostles; and some, prophets; and some, evangelists; and some, pastors and teachers; for the perfecting of the saints, for the work of the ministry, for the edifying of the body of Christ.
Ephesians 4:11–12 KJV

As a pastor, Karry Wesley was a counselor who gave guidance without alienating anyone. With a congregation as large as ours, he cared for us all. Once he interacted with you, his "computer mind" would record tidbits about you.

As a teacher, he taught us to care for and share with one another. "For to whom much is given, much is required" (Luke 12:48, paraphrased). He taught us to study, to read the Bible for ourselves. He taught us to be a witness from the Great Commission recorded in

Matthew 28. And in our going, he reminded us that God would be with us. He taught us to "bring all the tithes into the storehouse, that there may be food in My house" and to remember that the question is asked, "Will a man rob God?" (see Malachi 3:8–10 NKJV). Yes, in tithes and offerings. He taught us to love. "[Love] endures all things" (1 Corinthians 13:7 NKJV).

Pastor Bryan Carter told us on the Sunday immediately after Pastor Wesley went home to be with the Lord, to practice what he taught us.

This assignment has been difficult for me because my pastor transitioned on my seventy-ninth birthday—November 13, 2019. He was not just my pastor, but I knew him well enough for him to call me Mom. I referred to him as my child, and called him both Pastor and Son.

Cheryl called him Pastor, Honey, and other sweet names.

The boys called him Dad and Pops. The grandchildren called him Papa.

God called him Karry, My servant.

29

Doc

GREGORY KEITH SEALS

For everything there is a season, and a time for every matter under heaven: a time to be born, and a time to die; a time to plant, and a time to pluck up what is planted; a time to kill, and a time to heal; a time to break down, and a time to build up; a time to weep, and a time to laugh; a time to mourn, and a time to dance; a time to cast away stones, and a time to gather stones together; a time to embrace, and a time to refrain from embracing; a time to seek, and a time to lose; a time to keep, and a time to cast away; a time to tear, and a time to sew; a time to keep silence, and a time to speak; a time to love, and a time to hate, a time for war, and a time for peace.
Ecclesiastes 3:1–8 ESV

FOR ALMOST FORTY YEARS, Doc has been a part of my life and that of my family. He loved my family, and I love his. He was my pastor, he was my brother, and he was my friend. God allowed Karry Wesley to do an awesome work for the kingdom while here at Antioch, of which we have all been the beneficiaries.

For thirty-three years, Doc allowed me to utilize my gift and share my love of God's music here at Antioch. Whether it was at the Carr P. Collins Chapel on the campus of Bishop College, at the warehouse, 7408, or 7550 South Hampton Road, I am forever grateful, and I told him that. Through the years I found it astounding that he basically never shared his topics nor the scriptural basis for his sermons with me as I prepared music for the choir, but it seemed that we were always in sync. And oh, what mountaintop experiences we had!

Doc loved not only this church family, but all people. That is something that he had to help me with—loving all people. I recall early in the life of Antioch, one day Doc and I had lunch together, and we were discussing aspects of his vision and plans for the church. As he did so, I took the liberty to mention that there were some in the midst whom I felt were on the ship, but not with the ship, and needed to be kept under a watchful eye. I even went as far as to offer my services to smite some ears. I begged him, "Doc, let me cut them."

Doc sat back, took a deep breath, and after a minute said, "Gregory Keith, let's just pray for them."

I said, "Nah, Doc, I want to cut them."

But he said, "No, let's just pray for them." That was just the kind of man Doc was—kindhearted and compassionate.

I want to thank all of the children of Antioch who are now young adults who were raised here at Antioch. They have reconnected during the past few days via social media, sharing photos and memories of the years that were spent here under the pastoral leadership of Doc. Through their posts, they have taught me to not cry because his life is over, but to smile because it happened! Late the other night as I viewed some of the photos and the posts, I realized that it's those things I'll remember most: the smiles, the laughter, the learning, the growing, the good times and the bad, the mountaintop experiences, and even those rough journeys through the valley. And although it may be hard right now, it will be the memories of those things that will help us push away the pain and bring the smiles and laughter back again.

I was stuck in traffic the other day, and I had this thought of Doc. I could hear him clearly say, *Gregory Keith . . .*

> I loved my life and had great plans and dreams I would pursue.
>
> I loved to learn and loved to work—there was so much for me to do.
>
> But plans and dreams—as it always seems—are subject to delay,
>
> For life can bring surprises that take us from our way.
>
> I wanted to accomplish much—perhaps do something great—
>
> And though I have now moved along, I've learned it's not too late.
>
> There is a special part of me that today helps someone to live.
>
> I've done something great, I found a way to give.
>
> I am grateful I could help someone—I've left a legacy,
>
> So someone else can now live on, with just a little help from me.

Thank you, God. Thank you, Cheryl. Thank you, boys, for sharing Doc with us.

We now know and realize that in the end, it's not the years in your life that count—it's the life in your years.

Rest well, my pastor, my brother, my friend . . . until we meet again!

30

My Singing Pastor

JULIA GOLD

ALL HONOR AND GLORY to our heavenly Father for this day and for thirty-three unforgettable years of leadership from a true-to-heart man of God who used his wisdom, knowledge, and experience to improve the wellbeing of others, guide them with respect, and encourage them with love.

Please allow me to express and reflect on a few of the precious memories I have of my pastor, Dr. Karry D. Wesley.

I can recollect my first observation of Pastor Wesley back when he was a student at Bishop College. He and several of the theology students would attend Carver Heights Baptist Church, and when given the opportunity, they would preach your socks off your feet and set the roof on fire! Pastor Wesley was always a cool Camden, Arkansas, young man, decked out in his pressed black slacks, black and white houndstooth blazer, black tie, starched stiff white shirt, and his perfectly trimmed and shaped Afro. Oh yes, he was a looker, but above all, he was some kind of messenger bringing forth the word from the Lord.

At Carver Heights a few years earlier, there was a young junior female usher, Sister Cheryl, who, at about the age of twelve, caught my eye. I noticed her because she always seemed so spiritually mature and was a serious worshiper. Little did I know that as years passed, she would become the wife of this young man of God. Thus, Cheryl would become my first lady and Karry my pastor. I watched them grow up both physically and spiritually, while diligently, with devotion, accepting the responsibilities of leadership of the Antioch Fellowship Missionary Baptist Church. Simultaneously, they were establishing a home of love, birthing and raising three boys, furthering their education, and maintaining a secure and honorable marriage—all done God's way.

I will always cherish the opportunity Pastor extended to me to serve as the first director of music under his leadership. It was rewarding, yet quite challenging at times, especially when Pastor would call me up and say, "I would like to sing a number with the choir." He debuted with the mass choir, singing the lead on "Tell It." And yes, he sang from his heart, telling just how the Lord had truly blessed him to tell of His goodness, everywhere he went!

Well, we got through that one and he was "feeling his Cheerios." He called me again and said, "I'd like to do a number with the youth choir on their annual youth day."

His choice selection was "Jesus Can Work It Out," and again he sang from his heart, and the Lord truly worked it out! We were so blessed, but Pastor Wesley had worked me so hard with those two songs that I had to say, "Now Pastor, I really think you need to stick to preaching."

Throughout the years, Pastor ministered to me through his sermons and Bible study sessions. I like referring to them as "sermonic recipes" because the messages were always so timely. They seemed to be what was good for me and my circumstances. Whether it was a sweet or sour message, it was what I needed to hear and receive.

Pastor was a phenomenal man of discernment. I'll miss hearing him deliver those sermonic recipes, but he saw fit to leave more than one hundred sermons and books online for us to refer to for guidance. What a blessing!

I'll also miss tracking him down on Sundays after church, sometimes crossing the security boundaries, like going into Pastor's private parking garage. I would tell Casey Jones, "Hold up, hold up! I have to check on Sister Cheryl and Pastor to make sure he is following the doctor's care plan." He didn't always follow man's plan for him, but it is certain he followed the orders from the Lord. You know, we all make plans, but the Lord orders our steps.

I admired his broad spectrum vision for the church that extended beyond these walls. I admired his thoughtfulness and compassion for mankind, his sons in the ministry, the youth, and the senior saints, just to name a few.

Mostly, I truly admired how he openly showed his respect, devotion, and affection for his wife, Sister Cheryl, and his children. He never hesitated to let you know that if you offended one of them, you would have to answer to him.

He was a man of divine strength and courage, and he spoke with a strong voice of certainty and confidence. He truly loved the Lord. He was a saved man who answered God's calling to lead the people by the Holy Word, whether they liked it or not.

He was the son of Henry and Annie Wesley, who no doubt planted the seeds of faith in God deeply in the soil that yielded hope, love, compassion, and righteousness in their offspring, Karry Don Wesley. With these traits, Pastor ran the race and fought a good fight, as he would say, "Doing it God's way."

As I close, I will always remember the first Sunday in October 2019, when I entered the foyer of the worship center. Pastor was there doing what he always did, greeting the people as they were coming in. He appeared to be in the midst of a conversation, and since I did not want to interrupt them, I simply said, "Good morning, Pastor." Not really sure if he heard me, I kept walking.

All of a sudden, he yelled out, "*Hello-o-o*, Sister Julia." I stopped in my tracks and turned around to find him standing, smiling, and waving. I smiled and waved back to him. This scene just stuck in my mind. The Wednesday morning he passed, the Lord showed me that Pastor was saying hello to me with his voice, but bidding me farewell with his hand. That was our last earthly encounter.

To the Wesley family, the Antioch family, extended family, and friends, let's cherish the legacy Pastor Wesley has left us. Let's feast off the sermonic recipes, and there we will find the comfort and the strength that we all we need in this season and going forward.

May the Lord continue to bless all of you and hold you in the grip of His grace and His mercy. To God be the glory!

31

#AntiochRaised

LAKEISHA FIELDS

#AntiochRaised. That's me.

It all started in 1985—December 14, to be exact. I had the honor of being an usher in the Wesleys' wedding along with Cher Biggs, Brian Coleman, and Carl Sledge Jr. I knew the beautiful bride through my parents, who knew her and her family, but I do not recall knowing the groom. Well, let's just say that from that day forward, the groom and I formed a special bond.

From the age of seven, I have vivid memories of sitting in meetings and attending worship services in the Carl P. Collins Chapel at Bishop College, recollections such as watching Pastor preach every Sunday and then give the benediction as he would come down from the pulpit, stop, and get Sis Wesley to walk side by side down the long aisle to the main door to greet the congregation as they left worship service.

Shortly thereafter, we moved to 7408 South Hampton Road. This is where Pastor began to make a significant impact on my life. I had a great foundation at home with my parents; however, through Pastor's leadership, our church helped strengthen that foundation. I will never forget our youth activities that included annual days, revivals, trips, college tours, vacation Bible school, Baptist training union, the debutante and ambassadors program, young voices choir, Wesley cadets, summer youth program, attending the National Baptist Convention, rap sessions, and much more. Pastor Wesley was always there supporting and encouraging us.

He also made sure that we knew about the Christ he preached about Sunday after Sunday, and he encouraged us to accept Jesus Christ as our personal Savior and develop an intimate relationship with Him. During this time, I had not been baptized, and Pastor knew I wanted to be, but was scared. *Lord, you mean I have to get up and walk down the aisle and go down in the water?* He would assure me that everything would be okay. He even told me that he would come and walk with me when I was ready to make my decision, often looking my way as he extended the invitation to Christ. Well, in June 1991, after the sermon, the Lord gave me strength to get up and walk down the aisle.

There was only one thing different about this particular Sunday—Pastor was not there. Pastor Perry had preached and extended the invitation to Christ. Well, you know I heard about it when he got back! But I remember him being so excited that I had made that big step. He later baptized me, and I continued to serve. I always appreciated that moment in hindsight, because Pastor was concerned more about my salvation and not just my involvement.

While serving at 7408, I can recall him giving us so many opportunities. We were able to lead devotion, give the church announcements, co-teach Sunday school, plan programs and retreats, and sing, just to name a few. Not only was he encouraging us to serve and be actively involved in ministry, but he was equipping us for the future.

The week Pastor left us, some of the youth and former youth of Antioch had time to reflect on memories from 7408 and 7550. Memories like:

- Pastor singing "Jesus Will Work It Out" with the young voices;
- Pastor stopping in midsentence during his sermon and calling you out because you were talking too much during the service;
- Pastor walking through the halls to see if we were being on our best behavior for Bro. Tripp at SYP; or
- Doing what we called the Wesley stomp, where he would stomp three times and then turn back to look at the choir, or the famous Wesley hoop, where he would cross his arms and jump straight up and down; and then,
- That famous rap from Kool KD as youth graduated from high school.

Reflecting has helped some of us tremendously through this difficult time. We are thankful for the opportunities that we had to serve in the church under his leadership, we are appreciative of his support, as well as his corrective spirit, and we are grateful for the impact he has left on our lives.

To my Antioch-raised family, hold on to the memories. Continue to reflect on the times you had with him, whether at 7408 or here at 7550. Continue to look at and post pictures, but most of all, remember his teachings: the sermons, the conversations, the life he lived before us, and of course, just being there. Let's make him proud, and most importantly, let us please God by having a personal relationship with God, telling others about Christ, and being actively involved in ministry wherever you are.

To Sis Wesley, Chris, Karl, Charles, and the entire family—you all know that I love you. Thank you for sharing him with me, with us. Remember that God is your strength, and He will be with you now and in the days to come. Keep the faith. We will continue to lift you and the Wesley family in prayer.

I am #AntiochRaised. Thank you, Pastor, for the memories.

SECTION VI

Ministry Sons

32

When a Father Speaks

DR. ROD JONES

"ROD, YOU ARE A minister's minister." These are the words spoken to me by Dr. Karry Don Wesley. When he spoke these words to the heart of this pastor, it was well before I was even given the auspicious task of leading a group of people to the throne room of grace. My head and my heart dropped because he saw something in me that almost haunted me. When Pastor Wesley spoke these words, something in my soul began to resonate because that is the way I saw myself.

The reason why this is so important is because, unbeknownst to Pastor, I was engulfed in a personal struggle with the impetus of doing something outlandish for a great, magnificent God. This very notion prompted questions like, *Could this be of God, or is this my own arrogant flesh rearing its ugly head?* I was trying to make sure that I was operating according to the will of God and not the will of Rod. So when Dr. Wesley spoke these words, I could only but drop my head and ask, *Okay, Lord, where do we go from here?* Now I knew this was not of me, this desire to preach with a pristine power and the precision of a polished puppeteer. I knew the call of God was ushering me to yield to Him and to say, as the young Samuel said to God after being prompted by his master Eli, "Speak, for Your servant hears" (1 Samuel 3:10 NKJV).

Pastor Wesley gave me an assignment to be the liaison between the other associate ministers and himself. What this did for me was to put things into perspective. Pastor had a way of training and teaching you incognito. He may not have sat down and rolled out a five-year plan of pastoral ministry for me, but he did strategically make moves to position me where he thought God was taking me. Repeatedly, you've heard many people say about Dr. Karry Don Wesley that he was a man of few words, but he was also a man of big actions.

All this began before I officially met Pastor Wesley. I was attending a prominent church in Dallas, and my family had begun going to the Antioch church. I slowly started attending Bible studies and Sunday morning worship. I began to hear Pastor Wesley use words like *messianic expectation* and *dichotomous situation*. Being one who loves the use of words, I fell in love with Pastor Wesley's preaching style. When he would preach, my ears would perk up like a hound dog. He was a scholar as well as a pastor. He had the unique ability to take a text and, with the fidelity of the biblical context, bring it into today's context and make the Bible come alive.

I remember when he preached a sermon talking about the woman who anointed Jesus's head with oil. He talked about the expensive oil that the woman purchased so that she could anoint Jesus. That was more than twenty-some-odd years ago, and I still can remember Pastor Wesley saying that she purchased it from the Jerusalem Bath and Body Works. That ability, which now this pastor knows as contextualization, had me salivating like a dog waiting for a bone. To see him do it time and time again, to take a text in the biblical context and bring it to a modern context, was riveting.

Hearing Pastor Wesley preach and teach was what I needed to grow in my relationship with Jesus Christ. The thing that I can remember Sunday after Sunday is that he would preach a text of Scripture with such fidelity that you could tell he actually believed it was exactly as he was saying. Because he believed what he was preaching, it helped me to believe also. He had the unique ability to give all in his constituency a little bit of what they needed when he preached a sermon. Pastor Wesley had the ability to preach to those who had taken a jaunt through the academy, those who loved the deep things of theology. But he also had the ability to make it plain. I remember sitting in Bible study one Wednesday night as he explained one of those technical words that is used in the academy. He said the reason he explains it is because of one of the mothers in the church. He said that he was preaching a sermon laced with the words from the academy, and one of the mothers in the church yelled out, "Make it plain, preacher!"

Sometimes when I'm feeling myself in my pulpit and using too much jargon from the academy, my wife will say to me, "I didn't understand anything you said."

I can hear Pastor Wesley in the voice of that mother of the church saying to me, "Make it plain, preacher!"

But not only could Pastor Wesley touch the mind of the theologian and scholar, not only could he touch the heart of a parishioner, but he also had the ability to shut the place down. Pastor Wesley was a preacher's preacher who knew how to close a message. The thing that I loved about Pastor Wesley is that he knew how to whoop, which is technically called intonations, but he would only whoop when the Spirit led him. That spoke volumes to me because that told me that he was led by the Spirit of God.

The other thing that still resonates with me as a young apprentice watching a master craftsman work his trade, is before he gave the benediction he would say, "Oka-a-ay." The thing that stuck out is the way he said okay. He said it in somewhat of a drawn-out way, which communicated a sigh of relief, knowing that he had honored his King in the way that he conducted the service.

This stuck out to me because he didn't sound preachy or pastoral; he sounded like a man who loved his God and knew he had served Him well.

LEAVE YOUR FATHER'S HOUSE

Pastor Wesley had given me an opportunity to preach in the second service on Sunday morning, which was the packed service. Deeply honored, I preached, but then something happened. I felt deep within my heart that my work at the Antioch church was done. Not knowing how to actually hear from God and to wait on His leading and guiding, I was ready to go out and conquer the world for Christ. I decided to venture out without the blessing of Pastor Wesley's guidance. Needless to say, for that short time that I was out there on my own, I was like a fish out of water. The worst thing was that I caused my family to struggle and strain because I didn't have a clear word from God to move out. You must understand I was ready to conquer the world for Christ. I was so ready that I had Bible studies at my home, and the only one who was there to hear me teach the Bible like a skilled, seasoned sage was my wife.

One morning as I was running football practice, a local pastor, Mike Simmons, came walking down on my football field. The ironic thing is that while serving as a liaison for Pastor Wesley, I had tried to meet with Pastor Mike at the Hillcrest Baptist Church, but never could. God brought him to me. As I shared with him my heart's desires in ministry, Pastor Mike began to share with me his desire to integrate his church. Pastor Mike gave me some advice that I am truly grateful for. He told me to go back to Antioch and sit under Pastor Wesley's teaching and wait on God.

Before we could go back on a Sunday, we attended the funeral of a family member at Antioch. I gave Pastor a big hug and said, "Pastor, I missed you."

He responded by saying "I know, Son. You and Ronnie come over to the house so we can talk." When we got there, Pastor and Sister Wesley welcomed us with open arms. We talked and he said in that Pastor Wesley voice, "Rod, come on back home, and let's see what God would have."

The first Sunday we got back to the Antioch church, there was excitement mixed with a sense of failure. I was glad to be home with people who knew and loved me and loved my family, but I felt like a failure. Sitting on the front row with the rest of the associate ministers enjoying hearing my pastor preach, I felt dejected and unworthy to be sitting there, and to be totally honest, I was angry.

When Pastor Wesley gave the invitation to Christ, he said, "Rod, get up!" He was instructing me to get up and help. With those words, Pastor was not only reprimanding me, but was restoring me. That was his way of saying, "Son, I know you went out on your own, but you are still my son. Welcome home!" The next week, to my surprise, he put me back into a Sunday school class and allowed me to teach again. It was there that I began to hone my skills as a preacher. If that wasn't enough, he allowed me to preach one Sunday evening. I made a public apology to my pastor for his graciousness and ability to be led by the Holy Spirit to restore a prodigal son.

After six months of getting back into the groove of things at Antioch, God revealed that my time was up. This time I was not going to mess it up. I went to Pastor Wesley and shared with him my heart and what was on the heart of Pastor Mike. This time I said, "Pastor, if you tell me no, I am not going anywhere. If you say yes, then I will go. But I want you to know that I am not moving without your approval."

Pastor Wesley responded to me, "Rod, this makes sense to me. I could tell by the way you were preaching last time that you're ready to preach to a different type of congregation. Remember, I told you that you are a minister's minister. Go; you have my blessing."

When God began to transition me from the Antioch Fellowship Missionary Baptist Church to Hillcrest Baptist Church, Pastor Wesley was pivotal in my getting positioned to do what God had called me to do. God, in His sovereignty and sense of humor, decided that I would move from a black Baptist church to a white Southern Baptist church that was founded in 1890. The only thing

I could do as God began to transition us to serve with our Anglo brothers was to say, "Really, God?" I had no clue.

A Gift from My Father

Years later I was pastoring a congregation in East Texas. "Pastor, we are looking into purchasing a van and spending somewhere around twenty thousand dollars. We are in desperate need." These are the words that I spoke to Dr. Karry Wesley as I was prompted by the Holy Spirit to inquire if a little church in Nacogdoches could find a van to meet its needs. I had tried to get in contact with Pastor Wesley four times previously, and each time I called, I would end up speaking to the lovely Sister Wesley. Growing frustrated, I told the Holy Spirit, *I have been obedient to what You have called me to do.*

I felt like the Holy Spirit was saying to my heart, *No you didn't; you talked to Sister Wesley. I told you to call Pastor Wesley.* We finally connected.

Unbeknownst to me, God and Pastor were already working on a plan. I was not asking Pastor Wesley for a van, but rather if he could provide guidance for us to acquire a van of our own for Nacogdoches Bible Fellowship. A couple of weeks after speaking to Pastor, my brother and sister, who still attend the Antioch church, came down to visit. Right in the middle of service, my brother interrupted me and literally led me to the front of the church, with the congregation following. Once there, I saw a van with "Nacogdoches Bible Fellowship" and "Dr. Rod Jones, Senior Pastor" printed on it.

We all began to cry out, scream, and shout for joy. God had truly given us a blessing! He rained down the manna from heaven in the wilderness and made a van show up out of nowhere. Our plan was to go the very next day to purchase a van for $40,000. The loan was already prepared for us to sign.

This is the type of man Pastor Wesley was—a man who would answer the heart's cry of the people. He may not have been a man of many words, but he was truly of man of big actions. My father in the ministry wanted to bless his son.

One of the things that was a staple at the Antioch church was the men's conference that Pastor planned. The final one that he administrated and attended, in September 2019, had something unique about it. It was obvious that something was going on because four of the facilitators were his sons in the ministry. This was special in the way everything unfolded before our very eyes. You could almost see God saying that this was his swan song. In true Pastor Wesley fashion, he had all the facilitators on the stage to recap what we taught in our sessions.

Everything was just awesome with this conference, and then all of a sudden at the end of the conference, he did it again. Another son of the ministry, Ed Johnson, who had planted a church in DeSoto, Texas, was surprised also at what our pastor was about to do. Pastor Wesley gave him a van for his ministry in order to bring people to the church that he had founded. The church began to grow, and he needed help. I couldn't help myself but to go over and grab his neck and cry with him. I was excited at what had just happened, and I knew how he felt. For Pastor Wesley to come alongside and give him a van at the men's conference touched all our hearts deeply.

Pastor Wesley was a man of few words, but big actions. This is the way he had done things all his life. This is the way he has left a legacy that cannot be duplicated. The legacy of Dr. Karry Wesley is something that is so awesome.

One of my heart's desires was to get my pastor to come preach at my church in Nacogdoches. I was telling Sister Wesley of my disappointment. She said something that was so profound in the way that only Sister Wesley could say it. She said, "Rod, he's there." I was a bit befuddled as she was saying these words. She continued, "Because you are there, he is there."

I couldn't help but to say, in the words of my father in the ministry, "Look at God!"

33

Fatherhood Requires Love, not DNA

PASTOR BRANDON WALKER

I WAS THIRTEEN YEARS old when my family and I first moved to Dallas. I came from a small church in Houston and was like a son to my pastor. Growing up in a church where everybody knew everybody and with the pastor being like a father to me made my arrival at Antioch quite unnerving. I feared that I would get lost in the crowd. *What if I don't really make any friends? What if I never get to meet the pastor? If I do meet him, will he even remember my name?*

Well, not only did I get to meet my new pastor, but he remembered my name because he called me son, and I was proud to call him Pops.

Pops was one of a kind. He was a mysterious man. Nothing about him made sense. He pastored a huge church, but had such a humble spirit. He was invited to preach for some of the biggest churches and names in the country, but he preferred being at his church and with his family. He had an earned doctorate, but preached and taught in a way that even a seven-year-old could understand. He could preach for an hour in the pulpit, but could sit at home right across from you and not utter a word. He was never flashy. He loathed attention. And I rarely saw him eat anything other than fried chicken or fish.

Pops taught me so much. He taught me that family is my first ministry. He was just as serious about being at his son's games as he was about being at church. And it was nothing for him to sneak away out of town with Mama. As a matter of fact, I remember when I stayed in the Wesley household. One particular Sunday after church, we all went home, ate, and went to sleep. By the time we (the boys) woke up and went downstairs, he and Mom had caught a flight to New Orleans. We were all confused. But that was Pops. Being a partner and parent mattered just as much to him as being a pastor.

Pops taught me how to serve. Anyone who's attended a funeral at Antioch will tell you that it's a unique experience. Why? Pops. After delivering powerful eulogies, he'll go to the multipurpose center, take off his suit jacket, put on an apron, and help serve food. This was for anybody, whether you had been a member for thirty years or thirty minutes. He exemplified the term "servant leader." He also mastered the art of serving in silence. It seemed like every time I walked into his study, there was a new award for some contribution made to an organization. The crazy part is, he probably didn't attend the ceremonies for half the awards he received. He served to show he was paying attention to people. He never served for people to pay attention to him.

Pops also taught me the importance of handling God's Word correctly. The time he spent in God's Word showed every time he would speak. He left no stone in the text unturned. He took his call to preach the gospel seriously. One of the biggest compliments I've ever received was from him concerning my preaching. One Saturday he asked me to stand in his stead the following Sunday (yes, as in the very next day). His instructions were specific: "Be ready to preach for about thirty minutes tomorrow." I preached that Sunday. However, it wasn't thirty minutes.

There's something about being in the moment that makes you lose track of time. I'll never forget the text he sent me that afternoon: *That was a good sermon, but you didn't follow instructions. I said thirty minutes.*

All I saw was, *That was a good sermon.* Knowing that he liked my sermon was all I needed.

I really could go on and on, but there is one memory that summarizes how much I loved and respected him as my pops. I was fifteen. Every summer, we have what is called Summer Sessions with the Sons Sharing. These sessions are Sunday evening services where the associate ministers of the church are given the opportunity to preach. When we first started them, we had to create a manuscript of what we planned on preaching and send it to Pops for review beforehand. One day, in the middle of the week, he realized he hadn't selected anybody for the upcoming Sunday (are you seeing a pattern here?). He saw me and volun-told me to preach that Sunday.

I asked him, "When do you want me to send you my manuscript?"

He replied, "Don't worry about it. I trust you." This spoke volumes to me! It didn't make me feel good about who I was, necessarily. It actually made me love and appreciate him more.

You see, a son expects his father to love him, but you have to earn your father's trust. A father who trusts his son does so because he has been intentional in teaching, encouraging, correcting, and observing his son. He knows what his son is capable of, even if the son doesn't know himself. He is sure of his son's ability because he's sure of what he has poured into the son. He knows that what he has taught and given the son works, and if the son simply practices what he's been taught, he'll be fine. Pops taught me well. He instilled great things within me, and he was confident that I would do only what I'd been taught.

So when I stand to preach, I preach the way Pops taught me. When I lend a helping hand, I do so cheerfully and discreetly because that's how Pops did it. Every moment I share with my wife, I'm doing my best to love her the way Pops showed me to love your wife. Pops didn't teach me with his lips alone. He taught me with his lifestyle, and seeing him live it is what makes me want to really live that way.

The wonderful part about all this is that Karry Don Wesley was not my "real" pops, but he was a real pops!

34

A True Example

RUSSELL DABBS

As I reflect on my relationship with Pastor Wesley, several things and moments come to mind. I met him when I was just fourteen years old. I was always intrigued with the way that he carried himself. He was always astute and well versed. That stuck out to me.

Pastor Wesley meant so much to me. He was an example of true manhood. He was a man of few words, but those words always spoke volumes. I can remember sharing with him my thoughts about topics, whether it was biblically related or just simple life issues, and he would always give a good, sound response that was rooted in the Word of God.

He shared some very important milestones in my life and was there for me during some of the most difficult times. He didn't judge, nor was he one-sided.

He was a man of integrity. He did everything in excellence. He instilled that same quality in me. He loved his wife, and I am striving to do the same. He taught me about hard work, but also not to forget your first ministry, which is your family.

I will always be indebted to Karry Wesley.

35

My Role Model

PASTOR NYAL BELL

A N EXCERPT:

> I am very privileged and honored to be cho-
> sen to induct my dad into the Pro Football Hall
> of Fame. This is an historic event which my father,
> Walter, and members of the Payton family will trea-
> sure for the rest of our lives. His friends and fans
> will recall this memorable occasion. My dad had
> played football for thirteen years only missing one
> game and breaking all running back records. Not
> only is my dad an exceptional athlete, he is a role
> model. On behalf of your friends and your fans,
> I say congratulations! Thank you. (Jarrett Payton,
> Pro Football Hall of Fame, July 31, 1993)

I am very privileged and honored to be chosen to speak regard-
ing my mentor as he is inducted into the Hall of Faith. This is an
historic event that my spiritual father, Karry D. Wesley, and members of the Antioch family will treasure for the rest of our lives. His

family, friends, and fans will recall this memorable occasion. Dr. Wesley pastored for thirty-four years, rarely missing a Sunday and blessed us every Sunday. Not only was he an exceptional divider of the Word of Truth, but he is my role model. On behalf of your friends and your fans, I say congratulations! Thank you.

Subsequently and in retrospect, Jarrett Payton stated that had he made the introduction again, he would simply say, "Walter Payton, enough said," and drop the mic.

Likewise, I say, Dr. Karry D. Wesley—enough said.

SECTION VII

Pastor's A-Team

36

More Than a Boss

MARIE BROWN (FOR LERITHA, TIFFANY, BILLIE, KATIE, LAKEITA, JUSTIN, ABE, DREW, DONALD, ROBERT, AND SEAN)

JULY 1996, IN THE library at 7408, I sat down to interview with a panel of five individuals for the position of church secretary. They drilled me with so many questions that I found myself wondering, *Who is this man whom I am applying to work for?* Little did I know, God was setting me up to serve one of His great men of faith.

It is no exaggeration that Pastor was a true man of God. His life was a genuine example of a man seeking after God. And he has made a lasting impression in the life of every member of this staff. There are not enough words to describe the magnitude of his impact. To us he was more than just our pastor and boss. He was a good friend, brother, and confidant, and we all developed our own special bond with him. He was a servant leader who shared in the joys and pains of both our lives and his—in and out of the work environment. He shared like hobbies with some of us: gardening with OB, fishing with Pastor Cooper, and bowling with Leritha. As a staff, we saw him diligently pursue righteousness, godliness, faith, love, steadfastness, and gentleness. He was our leader. But like Billie would say, "He was more than a boss or a pastor, he was *family*."

Through the week, when he came to the church, he made his rounds to every office to speak to every staff member who was present. There were some offices where he would sit and visit for a while. In his walks through the building, we could hear him coming because of the outbursts of laughter from each of us as he would give us his daily dose of Karry Don with those famous Pastor one-liners, as Dr. Katie would say.

He was comical and cordially accommodating. One day, he, Casey, and I were sitting in his front office in a meeting. The door was unlocked, and in comes Billie right up in the middle of our meeting. She stands at the desk and says, "Oh, are you all having a meeting?"

I said yes, but Pastor said, "Nah, Billie, what do you want?"

She said, "Well, next time lock the door."

We all just fell out laughing. Needless to say, that was the end of that meeting, because he wanted to accommodate Billie.

He was a true scholar and loved the Word of God, and he would always encourage us to read the chapter in its entirety whenever he shared the Word. As I would transcribe his sermons, he would have more than fifty points to one sermon before condensing them. We could ask him questions about the Word, or life, and he would answer in ways we wouldn't have imagined. But he was usually not a man of many words. As Keita would say, sometimes he would give very short replies. But we all learned quickly that he was a man of deep thought and prayer. He would let us rant and rave while he looked at the floor, glancing up every now and again to show we had his attention. When we were finished going on and on, he'd look up and say, "I'll be praying." Then a quick, "All righty, then," and just that quick, he'd be gone.

Pastor was a selective leader and managed the staff as Jesus did His disciples—according to our temperaments and personalities. He listened intentionally to all our complaints and concerns, processing the need, and afterward imparted wisdom and truth accordingly.

He had the uttermost trust and confidence in this staff. Sometimes he would arrive at the church, walk in the office, and instruct me to call certain staff members to come to his office for a brief meeting. We would all put our agendas aside, and once we were gathered around the conference table, in a matter of minutes, he would share his ideas or some plan he was considering. Then he would say to us, "You all work it out and get back with me." It was just the turnaround time that would often throw us into a whirlwind because he would want it yesterday. But we were always ready to go the extra mile whenever duty called.

He trusted us to carry out the task assigned to our hands. He allowed us to be creative and operate in our area of giftedness. And he trusted us to complete it. We might have restless nights and skinned knees, but we got it done. We never wanted him to lose his trust or confidence in us. We were like children who wanted to please their father and make him proud. We all loved him, and he loved us.

Pastor encouraged growth and supported our personal and professional endeavors, whether it was attending school to pursue a higher education, attending seminars and conferences to better equip us to do our jobs, sharing ministry ideas and implementation, planning to run for an official status, pledging to a fraternity, or even buying candy or raffle tickets from our children or grandchildren. He was a supportive leader and champion with the highest respect for the family unit. He respected our spouses and loved our children and grandchildren. A true family man, he believed in putting family first, and he taught us to do the same, like when he rearranged his schedule to eulogize Keita's dad at his funeral.

Pastor was truly one of a kind. We will miss his quiet wisdom, as Dr. Katie mentioned, always remaining a trusted advisor and mentor. Personally, I will miss those days sitting in his library, with him sitting behind his desk and me in the armchair, going over calls to return, invitations to accept, regrets to send, books or presentations to prepare for Bible study and teaching engagements, and the discussions about his sermon points and illustrations, which affected my life. Most of all, I will miss those times when we just sat to catch up on our individual lives. All these moments are engraved in my heart.

I am eternally grateful for the opportunity to have served as his administrative assistant for twenty-three years. He was an incredible boss. This year for Boss's Day, he was battling his sickness, so I sent him this simple quote that depicts just what I felt about him as a boss. It said, "A truly great boss is hard to find, difficult to part with, and impossible to forget." I believe I speak for the entire Antioch staff when I say we found that truly great boss in the person of Dr. Karry D. Wesley. He was great in his leadership, great in his support, and great in his faith and love for the Lord, his family, this staff, and the entire Antioch family of faith.

Cheryl, Chris, Karl, Charles, Jasmine, Kamden, Karter, Kyrin, and Baby Marlei, thank you for sharing him with us. We already miss his presence in these hallways, hanging out at the information desk on Sunday morning with his trusted companion, Casey. They were inseparable. We already miss his presence sitting among us in staff meetings or at our staff lunches.

Hebrews 13:7 (ESV) says, "Remember your leaders, those who spoke to you the word of God. Consider the outcome of their way of life, and imitate their faith." There were times when Pastor would send his sermon points for the screen, and he felt like he would not be able to cover them all. In the email message he would say, "I am not sure which ones I will skip." Then in parentheses he would say, "So just follow me."

He may not have been sure about the points he was going to skip in his sermons or in this life, but he was sure about where he was going—heaven. And I believe his final words to us would be, "Just follow me."

37

Close Enough

FRANK DANIELS

A PROLIFIC MAN WHO bore so much knowledge and wisdom. A leader whom all can mimic in life. A preacher full of the Holy Ghost. A man who preached with conviction before, during, and after his illness.

I met Dr. Karry Don Wesley sixteen years ago as a new member to the church, not sure what my role would be or how I would fit in and serve at Antioch. The uncertainty was short-lived after getting involved in ministry, connecting with the brotherhood, and later becoming an ordained deacon. Those were a few proud moments, but the greatest of all was the bond created and the closeness shared with Pastor Wesley.

My favorite ministry was pastoral detail team, a.k.a. PD. Serving in this capacity brought joy and delight to be a supporter of such a great man. My responsibilities were small, but humbling. It was my responsibility to ensure that his iPad was charged and ready for service. It was always my fear that something would happen to the iPad while in transport from his office to the pulpit. I enjoyed slow-trailing him from afar, but close enough to reach him in case of any emergency or situation as he greeted members and visitors in his path. He was a stranger to none, loved all, and was a cornerstone who was loved by many.

Some of the fondest memories I gravitated to and admired:

- He was a family man who loved his wife, children, and his greatest joy, his grandchildren. I recall receiving a text from him that was meant for his wife; yes, it was clean! The text solidified my thought about the love he had for his wife.
- I recall returning home from deployment for rest and recuperation (R and R). Pastor Wesley and Sis Cheryl thought enough of my wife and me to have dinner with us, which made us feel very special.
- As grandfathers, we often shared grandparent stories. He had three grands at the time, and we had five grands. Pastor would regularly check on me and my wife to ensure that we were okay. One year he blessed the grands with State Fair of Texas tickets, and the kids had a blast.

Some people may describe me as an introvert, but I could go to Pastor with every concern, knowing that it was safe and secure. He would always end the conversation with godly counseling. His message was short and to the point, but it spoke volumes.

Not only was he my pastor, but he was my friend. I will truly miss him, and I will forever remember the great times we shared together. This transitional period has been hard, but "We know that all things work together for good to those who love God, to those who are the called according to His purpose" (Romans 8:28 NKJV).

Thank you, Pastor Wesley, for time served until we meet again.

38

Serving Pastor, Serving People

REV. JEFF JACOBS

I AM JEFFREY JACOBS, one of the sons of the ministry under the late Dr. Karry Don Wesley. Years ago when Antioch was located at 7408 South Hampton Road, I served as an usher. I would always serve in the same spot over by the loud drums, senior citizens area, and where Pastor entered the sanctuary. One Sunday as Pastor Wesley was about to enter the pulpit, he stopped and asked me a question. He asked, "Why do you always usher in the same spot?"

I said, "So I can take care of the senior section. I can see everything that's going on inside the church, and I can watch you."

Years later, I surrendered into the preaching ministry. I asked Pastor if it was okay for me to continue ushering until I was given an assignment. Pastor said no. He said he had something else for me.

As the church transitioned over to Paul Quinn College as the new church was being built, Pastor Wesley had a vision. His vision was to bring men together who were not serving and place them alongside the ones who were. The challenge was great, but through discussions and prayer, we were able to form the armor bearer ministry. Casey Jones was the assistant to Pastor Wesley, I was the manager of the armor bearers, and Terry Listenbee was the trainer.

We used much prayer and Scriptures like Ephesians 6:10–24 (KJV):

> Finally, my brethren, be strong in the Lord, and in the power of his might. Put on the whole armour of God that ye may be able to stand against the wiles of the devil. For we wrestle not against flesh and blood, but against principalities, against powers, against the rulers of the darkness of this world, against spiritual wickedness in high places. Wherefore take unto you the whole armour of God, that ye may be able to withstand in the evil day, and having done all, to stand.
>
> Stand therefore, having your loins girt about with truth, and having on the breastplate of righteousness; and your feet shod with the preparation of the gospel of peace; above all, taking the shield of faith, wherewith ye shall be able to quench all the fiery darts of the wicked. And take the helmet of salvation, and the sword of the Spirit, which is the word of God: praying always with all prayer and supplication in the Spirit, and watching thereunto with all perseverance and supplication for all saints; and for me, that utterance may be given unto me, that I may open my mouth boldly, to make known the mystery of the gospel, for which I am an ambassador in bonds: that therein I may speak boldly, as I ought to speak.
>
> But that ye also may know my affairs, and how I do, Tychicus, a beloved brother and faithful minister in the Lord, shall make known to you all things: whom I have sent unto you for the same purpose, that ye might know our affairs, and that he might comfort your hearts.

Peace be to the brethren, and love with faith, from God the Father and the Lord Jesus Christ. Grace be with all them that love our Lord Jesus Christ in sincerity. Amen.

We prayed around the church as it was being built. We fellowshipped together. Now we serve the members at Antioch Fellowship with wheelchair assistance, sickness, nurse assistance, valet parking, and anything else necessary to keep the flow of the church moving smoothly. We also build our spiritual relationship with God as we serve. Pastor's vision is at work at Antioch.

After Pastor passed, my daughter asked me what I will do now that the person I protected is no longer here. At first I said, "I don't know." After thinking about my answer, I said, "Pastor was not the first spiritual leader I had. I also had my mother and my father, and they all left something for me in my spirit—to continue serving God."

I give thanks to God for allowing my pastor to put me in an uncomfortable position to serve His people.

Thanks, Pastor Wesley.

39

My Trusted Friend

O. B. PORTER

I MET PASTOR WESLEY when we joined Antioch in December of 1990. As we spent a lot of time together at the church, we realized that we had a lot in common. I guess you could consider us old school. Our conversations were filled with us sharing our love for our God, our families, our jobs, gardening, landscaping, and other things as well.

I have had a lot of health issues over the years. Whenever I was going through some of my experiences, Pastor Wesley, after preaching two or three sermons on Sundays, would always call to check on me. That meant a lot to me. We trusted each other with our hearts and our families. I trusted my family with the Wesley family, and he trusted his family with the Porters. That included both immediate and extended family.

I respected his leadership as a boss, and he was very respectful to me as an employee. When it came to personal gardening and landscaping, we would always share ideas. He knew that he could count on me to support him with his various projects he wanted to get done. He really loved sharing his stories about his fishing trips. Yet there was a lot of time we would be in the same space for hours and not feel obligated to say a word to each other. There also was a season when we would go camping and bowling with other friends. Those times were priceless.

I guess what I will miss most are the opportunities to share life experiences with him as we have done over the years. In our communications, whether it was talk or text, we knew that whatever was said to each other would remain there. I thank God I was blessed to have had him as a trusted friend.

40

Tribute to My Brother

JOEL LEACH

WHEN I FIRST JOINED Antioch almost twenty years ago now, I didn't want or desire to have a close relationship with the pastor. It was not that I didn't like or had something against Pastor Wesley, but it was primarily because of my past experience of being up close and personal with the pastor of my prior church. When God led us to unite with Antioch, it was my desire to attend church regularly, fly under the radar, and not be involved. Well, fortunately, God had another plan for me as I became involved in the armor bearer ministry and the men's ministry. It was through those ministries that I developed a close and personal relationship with Pastor Wesley.

Developing a relationship with Pastor Wesley was indeed what I needed. For a time, I shied away from developing close relationships with and bonding with men as I was still heartbroken from losing my two best friends, who were also the best men at my wedding. Both died in a three-month span in 1999, and I was still reeling from that when I joined Antioch. Once I became involved in ministry at Antioch, it appeared that wherever I was, somehow I would always cross paths with Pastor Wesley. When our paths would cross, he'd always want to talk to see how I was doing, how the kids were doing, and if things were okay with Roz and me. From there, our relationship blossomed to conversing about the challenges of raising sons.

The more we talked about life, the more we both realized that we had a lot in common and, to some degree, were a lot alike. We both enjoyed fishing and sports. We discovered that we both were introverts. A lot of times we'd attend events, and as people would socialize and move through the crowd, it was common for Pastor and me to be in a corner somewhere, just the two of us, talking and people watching.

Over the years, our relationship grew closer and we became brothers. Brothers to the point where we became each other's confidants. Brothers to the point that we talked or texted daily. Brothers to the point that we could privately tell each other, Hey, brother, you're wrong on that; you probably can handle this or that better. Brothers to the point that we knew what the other was thinking before either of us said anything. Brothers to the point where we expressed our love for one another by saying, I love you, brother. In my last conversation with Pastor, which I relive daily, we laughed and talked for more than an hour. At the conclusion of the conversation, he grabbed my arm, pulled me closer to him, and said, "Brother, you know I really love you."

Having a close relationship with Pastor propelled my desire to be an even better Christian husband, father, man, and servant. Having a front row seat observing him made me a better man. Pastor was not only my pastor and brother, but he was also my accountability partner. Pastor knew that I traveled quite a bit for work. When I would be out of town for work, he'd always call me at weird hours and say, "You were in my spirit and on my heart. I just wanted to check in with you to make sure you were good and that you remember whose you are."

As I close before I become too emotional, the quality that I most loved about Pastor was his ability to look at me and say, "I don't know what's going on with you, but I know that something is going on. Whatever it is, it's nothing that God can't handle." After that, he'd grab my hand, go to God in prayer, and then call or text me until I would tell him that all was well. In this life, we all need friends who encourage us, support us, are honest with us, love us unconditionally, and pray with and for us. Pastor was that kind of brother and friend to me! I miss him dearly!

41

Service to My Dear Friend

CASEY D. JONES II

MEETING PASTOR KARRY D. WESLEY

I BEGAN VISITING ANTIOCH Fellowship Church the summer of 1988, but I was extremely reluctant to become a member of a large, growing church congregation. Because of this, I would just come on Sundays, sit in the back of the church, and occasionally attend the Bible study sessions on Wednesday evenings.

I found the pastor of this church (that I would not join) to be uplifting and to deliver messages that spoke to my spirit like no other minister I had heard before. The pastor spoke in a modern tone that dealt with issues that resonated with my generation. I was used to the old-school church where only the older members ran everything and the pastor only spoke to that generation. However, this pastor was different and unique with his preaching delivery and teaching. This guy was doing things like matching words in the delivery of his sermons. For example, he would have bullets like "The Practical Purpose, The People Participating," and his entire sermon would be written and delivered in that format. The first time I heard him speak, I was so amazed how he put the message together and stayed so practical in the Word. He dissected the Scripture so intelligently that I began to question some of that old-school church that would put me to sleep as a child and teenager.

At this point, I started to attend Antioch Fellowship more on a regular basis and became a regular attendee at Bible study on Wednesday evenings. In fact, I would attend the Bible study sessions more than attending church on Sundays. The teaching of this pastor was exhilarating. I learned more about the Word attending Bible study for six months than I had for my entire life (twenty-five years of age), but at this point I had still not even personally introduced myself to the pastor or his spouse. I was just using the Antioch church for my spiritual growth, hitting the exit before anyone would notice me, and not giving a dime to the program.

Then one day it hit me. *I think I want to finally have my own church home. Not one my mother made me attend as a child that never really spoke to my spirit, but a church family where I could grow and raise my family.* So on Wednesday, July 10, 1991, I finally joined Antioch Fellowship during our Bible study session and came down front to meet the pastor, Karry D. Wesley. As I came down front, Pastor greeted me stating, "Welcome to your church home, Bro. Jones." I was outdone that this dude knew my name. I had been attending the church for a few years now, but not really connecting with anyone, and had never been within ten feet of the pastor.

The next week at the conclusion of the Bible study session, the pastor invited me to his office for a conversation. I thought I was in big trouble after only one week as an official member. Remember, at this point I had not given one penny to the church, so I thought maybe I was about to be called on the carpet for that or something else. Here I am, this single man (engaged to Karen), a member of this growing church, and I am in the pastor's office just one week after joining. *Did I get caught checking out one of the sisters?*

Turns out, our first official conversation was amazing. Pastor first asked me why I joined Antioch and why the delay in joining. I informed him of my thought process, and he was extremely understanding. Then the conversation turned more personal. We found out that we shared a lot in common; we both have family rooted from Arkansas, and some of those family members grew up together. We talked about this church and his vision; we talked about his family, spouse, and two boys; and we talked about my engagement to Karen Banks. Karen and Pastor both attended Bishop College during the same period, so that coincidence was another point of conversation. I cannot tell you everything Pastor and I talked about that night, but to give you an idea of how detailed it was, Pastor and I engaged in conversation for more than two hours after Bible study was concluded.

Pastor and I did not talk every day, but we did hit it off. We were becoming fast friends. However, very seldom did we talk about Antioch Fellowship or church in general. Our conversation was mostly related to family, sports, my engagement, etc.

Karen and I were married in June 1992. Karen would immediately join Antioch Fellowship and become a member of the church family. Karen and Cheryl would begin to build their own friendship as part of the Antioch Lydia Mission Circle. Karen, Yunatrice Porter, and Cheryl were like the Supremes—when you saw one, you saw the other two. Pastor and I were already very good friends, but when our spouses became good friends, the Wesley-Jones friendship blossomed. Along with the Porter family, we all began to hang out, take vacations together, etc.

At the time, Karen and I were the only couple without children, so we had the ability to watch and learn the amazing parenting skills of the Wesley and Porter families. For example, I remember one trip during the summer of 1998. We all decided we would visit Sea World in San Antonio, Texas. Charles was just three at the time. The Porter, Wesley, and Jones families made the eight-hour trip and arrived at Sea World. Once arriving at the Sea World ticket gate, Pastor and OB glanced at the prices and noticed that children under two years of age could enter the park for free. I saw Pastor and OB over there plotting, and I decided to enter the conversation. Pastor called the play: "Casey, you hold Chris and Karl's hand. I am going to put Charles on my shoulder, and we will get him in for free." That's just one example, but there are so many others. We would go camping, fishing, or, when needed, just a weekend away as brothers.

I am not a fisherman at all. I have no desire to ever actually go fishing, so imagine my surprise one day when Pastor asks me to go fishing—just the two of us. Pastor knows I do not fish; he knows that I don't even know how to bait a hook. Besides, Pastor likes to fish alone or with another person who has a passion for fishing. It's his quiet time. I knew the invitation meant that Pastor wanted to talk, and the fishing would be secondary.

So we drive down to some small pond only he knows about, talking during the two-hour trip. Once we arrive and unpack all the fishing gear, Pastor leads us to a particular spot on the pond to begin fishing. We are joking and laughing because Pastor must bait my hook for me. Well, we are out by the pond for hours, and Pastor has not caught anything, and I am cool with just holding my pole and waiting for that little red thing in the water to move.

By this time, Pastor has moved to another area of the pond because where we were sitting, he has not caught a fish. As soon as Pastor gets settled in another area, that little red thing connected to my pole goes under water, and I am fighting whatever is pulling on my pole. Pastor runs to where I am by the pond, yelling at me to not let it go, and then begins to encourage me to bring the fish in. It was a large bass—the only fish we caught that day.

I will never forget this day. It may not seem like much, but it was a day when he really needed to talk and wanted an objective opinion on a host of issues.

Pastor Karry D. Wesley's Armor Bearer

I am often asked, "How did you become Pastor's armor bearer?"

Shortly after joining the Antioch Fellowship Church, I began to explore areas where I could get involved in the ministry. I became a member of the finance team, participated in a few other ministries, and continued with Wednesday evening Bible study. In 1993, Pastor asked Karen and me to join him and Cheryl on a trip they were taking to Camden, Arkansas, for a preaching engagement he was to facilitate at the Zion Hill Baptist Church. Donald and Crystal Perry would also join us on the trip.

Once we arrived at the church, Donald and I noticed that no one was there to serve Pastor and Cheryl. As a result, I just hung around to see if there was anything needed, and it blossomed from there. When we arrived back at Antioch Fellowship the next Sunday, I began serving in that capacity with no official title or role. Donald and I would just make sure Pastor's needs were met before preaching on Sundays. Eventually I resigned from the finance team, and Donald was leading other ministries as an associate minister. It was Pastor who asked me to serve as his personal assistant, and the term "personal armor bearer" was born at Antioch Fellowship.

Eventually Pastor would ask me to expand the ministry. With the expansion, we created the congregational armor bearer team, the pastoral detail team, and the first lady detail team.

It has truly been a joy serving as Pastor's assistant. I have had a front row seat to all his sermons, speaking engagements, and accomplishments. There are so many things that stand out and so many stories I could tell.

For example, there was August 2005. Pastor was scheduled to facilitate a revival in Hattiesburg, Mississippi, to begin Monday, August 17. We arrived in New Orleans, Louisiana, on Sunday evening, August 16, to drive to Hattiesburg the next day. This was my first time driving from New Orleans to Hattiesburg, and I was not aware of the long bridge you had to cross over Lake Pontchartrain. This was fine during the day driving to Hattiesburg, but once the revival was completed on Thursday, August 20, Pastor decided we would head back to New Orleans that night so we would have enough time for rest for a Friday evening flight back to Dallas. During our stay in Hattiesburg, we had heard of news flashes with reference to Hurricane Katrina, but no one seem to be extremely alarmed about the storm, so we were not particularly alarmed. However, when we crossed Lake Pontchartrain Thursday night, it did not seem normal as the wind was high and water was flowing over the bridge. We made it back to New Orleans, and Pastor explored staying an extra day. We decided to stick with our schedule and depart Friday evening. Hurricane Katrina hit the Gulf of Mexico Sunday.

Words cannot express how much I appreciate our relationship. Pastor and I shared more than twenty-seven years, and I cherish every moment. If you were to ask me what I loved most about Karry D. Wesley, I would have to say the trust we had for each other. In twenty-seven years, not one of our private conversations was ever repeated.

Thank you, Dr. Karry D. Wesley.

42

Pastor's PA

DR. CAROLYN BRADLEY-GUIDRY

IN 1991, MY HUSBAND, Michael Guidry, and I joined Antioch Fellowship Missionary Baptist Church, under the leadership of Pastor Karry D. Wesley and First Lady Cheryl Wesley. This decision afforded me the opportunity to grow as a Christian, a wife, and a mother after Michael and I started our family. My family and I had a place where we could learn, develop, and align with God's will for our lives within a strong church community.

After we introduced our children to Christ, Pastor Wesley was there to nurture their spiritual growth. Some special family memories with Pastor include the blessing and baptizing of our daughters, Carinthia, Chassidy, and Chelsea; Carinthia being selected to participate in the ribbon-cutting ceremony to celebrate the official opening of our newly constructed church; and Pastor and Cheryl surprising Chassidy in Baton Rouge, Louisiana, when they attended her graduation from Louisiana State University Paul M. Hebert Law School.

Over the years I have served in various church ministries, including being the co-director of the medical response team ministry. I, along with other medical professionals, was tasked with providing immediate care to those in need during church services and special events. Little did I know that the medical ministry would be the catalyst for a closer relationship with Pastor Wesley, particularly as he allowed me to assist him during his medical journey.

One of my degrees is in physician assistant (PA) studies. However, Pastor transformed "physician assistant" to his own definition, which he referred to as his personal assistant (PA). I must admit, this was no easy task. Pastor was a very strong-willed man and believed in doing things his way and on his time. I worked diligently to assist him with his health-care needs. I helped him understand his diagnostic studies and treatment plan, provided feedback for medical points that he included in his video health updates and sermons, and encouraged him to comply with all medical recommendations. Some of our most challenging conversations were around dietary recommendations. Simply put, Pastor wanted to eat what he liked, regardless if it was recommended or not.

Pastor never wanted a lot of attention when he was not feeling well. Once during a church event, Pastor didn't feel well and requested that his blood pressure be taken by one of the medical response team members. I was out of town on the day of the event; apparently several nurses went to his aid. I received a text message from him later that evening stating, "Whenever I need help, I only want one or two people to help me. The medical team is excellent, but I do not need the entire ministry to help me; they need to be assisting the members." From that day forward, Pastor had two nurses assigned to him at all times, and of course he knew who they were. Pastor was always in charge and did not like surprises at all.

Speaking of surprises, when Pastor had his heart attack, unbeknownst to him, Cheryl called me to meet them at the hospital. When I walked into the hospital room, it was obvious Pastor was totally shocked to see me. The look in his eyes was clear—Cheryl had not told him I was coming. I said, "Hi, Pastor. Yes, I am here." A few minutes later the doctor came in, and I engaged in dialogue with the doctor; it became clear that Pastor was glad I was there to assist and facilitate the conversation.

Pastor Wesley was a humble, loving man and devoted teacher in all circumstances. Through his encounter with heart disease and his battle with cancer, he demonstrated and taught us how to worship through adversity. Through all that Pastor Wesley endured, I never once heard him complain or question God. Instead he would say things like, "I am still processing everything and praying during this season." According to Pastor, I was his personal assistant (PA), but instead of helping Pastor, I can honestly say I received more help from him than I was able to give. Pastor's medical journey allowed me to grow both personally and professionally. I believe I am a much better provider because of Pastor Wesley. I love him and will miss him dearly.

Pastor Wesley will forever be remembered and loved. He will never be forgotten.

.

SECTION VIII

A Pastor beyond the Walls

43

A Phone Call Away

RYAN BRADLEY

I WOULD LIKE TO start by thanking Mrs. Wesley, Chris, Karl, and Charles for granting me this wonderful opportunity to speak on behalf of Pastor Dr. Karry D. Wesley. I am so honored, and I love you all so much.

But with that being said, this is also one of the more difficult tasks I've been called on to do, and it's not because he's been called home after doing a wonderful job here impacting all our lives in a positive way, but because I can go on all day about how great a man he was.

Although I've been a member of Antioch for eighteen years, I actually met Pastor Wesley outside of the church. I was in the fifth grade, and my parents signed me up to play Little League football, which is where I met Karl. He was the quarterback, and I played receiver. I remember running back to the sideline after a touchdown, and all the parents would line up and give us high fives. Pastor Wesley would always say, "Great job, son." From there, I would always call him Pops. And let me tell you, at a young age you don't know too much, but you do have feelings, and I felt the love and care that he had for not just me, but for my family.

Karl and I had a lot in common growing up. We went to the same school and had the same classes. Both have an older brother in Ross and Chris, who also hold a very strong friendship. My brother was actually a groomsman in Chris's wedding. Both of our mothers worked for the school district side by side for ten-plus years, where they would become sisters for life. And we both come from strong black men who would do any and everything for their families as fathers. Now I didn't have a little brother, so thank you, Charles, for filling that spot in and always looking up to me like a big bro. You don't know it, but that little brother motivation took me a long way.

I remember coming to church throughout the years and just being so impressed with how Pastor was able to balance it all out, from being a man helping out in the community to being a great father to his kids, a great mentor and role model to all of us, a faithful husband and servant of the Lord, and still preach a great word each and every Sunday. He really changed my perspective on life. I no longer wanted to be like the athletes and famous people I would see on the television, but wanted to be more like the man whom I actually got to see in real life.

Pastor Wesley was always there for me. I'm going to fast-forward to December 2017. My grandmother, Emma Hodge, who was also a member of Antioch, got real sick with walking pneumonia and was called home at the age of seventy-five after being in the hospital for two weeks. I remember being so broken up inside. I had never experienced losing someone so close to me. I couldn't function. While at the hospital with my family, I received a call from Pastor Wesley just letting me know, "I'm right here, son. Whenever you need me, I'm here."

Five short months later, on April 8, 2018, on my oldest daughter's tenth birthday, I was sitting at home waiting on my mother to come back from running her errands. I got a knock on the door. There were officers from the Dallas Police Department standing there, informing me that my mother was in a bad car wreck and died instantly from the impact of the crash. Once again, I was broken up. Within hours, Mama Wesley was at the house. She hugged and held me while I cried on her shoulder. I'll never forget that hug. I could feel my mother hugging and kissing me goodbye for the last time. Moments later, Pastor called and told me to lean on him when I needed strength. He would say, "I'm right here, son. Whenever you need me, I'm right here."

Seven months later, in November 2018, my daughter was walking to her bus stop from school and was struck by a speeding car. Instead of stopping, the driver fled the scene, leaving my daughter with a broken jaw, broken ankle, and fractured femur. This left me once again hurt and confused. Within thirty minutes of sitting at the hospital, Karl showed up, hugged me, and handed me his phone. It was Pastor Wesley on the line telling me, "Hey, son, remember that God makes no mistakes. Stay strong and never lose your faith. I'm right here whenever you need me, son."

I'm going to close with this: for the past eighteen years, there have been two parts of church that I would always look forward to. First was the energy Pastor would bring to the room as soon as he would walk in, probably about midway through the second song. I would watch him as he would walk in, sit down in his chair, cross his legs, and nod his head while the choir sang. So cool and confident. He served God so well.

The second part was toward the end of his sermon, where he would ask the crowd his famous line, "Is there anybody here?" I would always answer in my head, *Yes sir, Pops.*

My two brothers, Chris and Brandon, preached at my mother's funeral. The message to me and my brother was that we would not drown. And trust me when I tell you, I'm swimming now, family, and it's because of Pastor and the Wesley family.

So let me leave my brothers Chris, Karl, and Charles with this: Whenever you think you are alone, think about Pop's line, "Is there anybody here?"

I'll speak for everyone in the building in response, just like Pops would. "We are right here, we will always be here, and we are not going anywhere."

Love you all, and God bless!

44

God's Justice Seeker's Journey

TERRELL D. BOLTON,
DALLAS'S FIRST AFRICAN AMERICAN POLICE CHIEF
(1999–2003)

Pastor Wesley and I knew each other for more than thirty years. During this time, Pastor Wesley and his family have occupied a special place within the hearts of my family. He was closer than a brother to me. We shared a Christian and historical walk together. Pastor and First Lady Sister Cheryl Wesley have always stood in the gap with respect to our children. They have been the best pastor and first lady team anyone could ever have prayed for and received. The Bolton family has been enriched by the relationship with the Wesley family.

Reflecting on my relationship with Pastor Wesley is consistent with the phrase "bitter and sweet." It is bitter from the standpoint that I miss him every day. While Pastor and I didn't communicate each day, week, or month at times, we shared a connection I believe God ordered. We were always there for God's plan. It is sweet from the perspective of hopefully blessing someone with good stories and deeds related to Pastor Wesley's justice-seeking role within the city of Dallas. He boldly embraced his godly position.

While there are countless stories related to the joyful and blessed times together at Antioch, I have been tasked with sharing experiences I had with Pastor Wesley as the civic and true community leader he was.

It's important that I outline the early history and dynamics of the Wesley and Bolton family relationship. As I look back, I believe God connected us for a historic mission together. It was not evident to me at the time. Pastor Wesley's early walk with me during the 1980s was a major factor of how he became the first secret holder other than my wife to know who would be announced as Dallas's first African American police chief.

I met Dr. Karry D. Wesley during the mid-1980s through an introduction from his wife, Cheryl Wesley. Pastor Wesley and I became friends immediately, and our bond grew stronger as we witnessed and experienced life's challenges in Dallas.

Sister Cheryl and I worked together during this time for the Dallas Police Department. Sister Cheryl held an important position within the Psychological Services Division. One may not be aware, but Sister Cheryl counseled gun-carrying police officers, civilian police department employees, fire department personnel, and their families. Also, Sister Cheryl was young, black, and female, which was a rare presence during this time to hold such a position. She was outstanding. Cheryl executed the demands of her position with precision, grace, empathy, and Christian love. I thanked God for her.

God had blessed me professionally during my tenure with the Dallas Police Department. I had scored well on promotional exams and received extensive executive training. My professional career had taken off. At the time that I met Sister Wesley, I was assigned as the administrative coordinator for the first African American assistant chief. The Psychological Services Division, where Sister Cheryl worked, along with the Personnel and Community Services Divisions, reported under this one management umbrella.

Dallas, like many major metropolitan cities during the 1980s, was struggling with challenging community and police relationships. Many of the same issues dealt with then persist today. During this time, Pastor Wesley was a young senior pastor at Antioch. The church was located at 7408 South Hampton Road. Dallas Police Department had received national attention for its use of deadly force. Twenty-nine citizens were killed or wounded within a year, most being African American. From 1980 to 1985, Dallas recorded more than 130 police-involved shootings. Sixty citizens were killed. These alarming statistics and community outrage mobilized leaders like Pastor Wesley to demand justice and accountability. A full congregational hearing was held in Dallas to examine this problem.

Pastor Wesley expressed ongoing concern to me. He was genuine and always had the community's interest at heart. He never expressed any concerns of whether a citizen was a member of Antioch Fellowship or not. Pastor subscribed to Dr. King's theory: "An injustice occurring anywhere is a threat to justice everywhere." He impressed me with his deep analytical thought process and his ability to be empathetic. He would pick up the phone or meet anywhere to address the issues of others.

While Dallas was going through this major challenge and controversy, the police chief personally reassigned me to city hall. I reported as a liaison between the police department and the community. I reached out to Pastor Wesley often for wisdom and God's guidance. He was always on point with encouragement and wisdom.

Dallas went through a major transition as Dallas's mayor and police chief changed. The outgoing chief, who mentored me, supported me. God continued to show me favor as the incoming chief embraced my professional efforts. He assigned me to Oak Cliff as their first African American deputy chief. The assignment covered the area where Antioch is located.

Pastor Wesley was happy with this development, and so was I. As I settled into the position, Pastor officially accepted my request for him to be the formal advisory member to the police department's southwest division. He worked tirelessly to pursue equal justice for all. The joy of coming to Oak Cliff as the deputy chief swiftly transitioned to meeting the challenges present upon my arrival.

There were several pressing issues. First, the Oak Cliff community was in the process of exploring how to secede from the city of Dallas. The second issue involved the Red Bird Mall being overtaken by juveniles daily, affecting its financial viability. The third issue involved auto thefts in the area, which ranked the highest in the city at the time. The last issue was local high school football players involved in a robbery spree that shocked the nation. Pastor Wesley never flinched. He trusted my discernment related to these issues and mobilized efforts to support the department's responses to these matters.

Pastor Wesley always planned ahead. Understanding the complexities of the challenges facing Oak Cliff, he consistently dispatched good men like the late Brother John Calloway to meetings. Brother Calloway and other Antioch members' presence served as an informative feedback channel for the congregation. After several months of formalized meetings related to the Oak Cliff secession initiative, the city of Dallas and the Oak Cliff community found common ground.

One concession from the city, among many made, was to add additional police officers within the community to help address its high crime rate. As Oak Cliff began to get those police resources, the area ultimately realized the most diverse police division within the city. Pastor Wesley called me and expressed his joy and optimism.

With regard to the Red Bird Mall juvenile loitering problem, Pastor Wesley participated in efforts to assist in eradicating this issue. Through community and police collaboration, parents were briefed and educated on the harm being done by them dropping their children off without supervision. Pastor Wesley's leadership and efforts bridged this important gap between police and community.

Oak Cliff's auto theft problem was abated with hard police work and community involvement. However, there was a tragic sacrifice for fighting this problem. We lost two young officers from the Southwest Station during a car theft police chase. Pastor Wesley provided much-needed wisdom and comfort to the department and the community during this tragic event. With God's help, we were able to get past this and come together as a community.

While experiencing some success, an unexpected, heartbreaking storm blew in. Several high-profile athletes were arrested for allegedly robbing businesses within the area. This incident captured national media attention and caused the community tremendous grief.

I personally knew one of the young men and his parents. I watched him grow up and attend church, and I couldn't reconcile why this occurred. I called Pastor C. B. T. Smith, who was the young man's pastor. I also notified Pastor Wesley and several other pastors within the community. They assisted the police department in its efforts to manage this unfortunate tragedy. Pastor Wesley assisted, as he always did. He placed strategic calls to arm individuals with specific information, which was important for community healing. This event ended tragically and resulted in several young boys being sentenced to prison.

When reading this reflection of my Christian walk with Pastor Wesley, one may assume that I was a member of Antioch. I actually was still a member at Golden Gate during this period, but would join Antioch years later, upon Pastor Smith's retirement.

I appreciated my relationship with Pastor Wesley and Antioch. I was impressed with Pastor's comfort in leading a church that understood the need for having an outward focus. Antioch always supported justice for all and demonstrated this principle by its strong community involvement.

Getting to know the members of Antioch was a blessing. When I was the deputy chief of the Oak Cliff area, Pastor Wesley regularly scheduled me to come out and speak to the membership. I always enjoyed fellowship and developed lifelong relationships that remain today.

As Dallas continued to evolve, police chiefs changed once again in 1992. The new chief arrived from California and assembled his staff. I was reassigned to lead the Internal Affairs Division downtown. While this was a blessing for my career, it meant that I wouldn't be leading the Oak Cliff area anymore. I knew I would miss my relationships and friends that I had made. No longer could I drop in on Pastor Wesley, Pastor Haynes, Pastor Smith, and all the other pastors whom I had grown to love and trust. I contacted Pastor Wesley and community leaders to inform them of my reassignment. I thanked them for their unwavering support.

As Pastor Chris Wesley preached recently, I was in the midst of an unusual process. Interestingly, Pastor Chris was three years old at the time, while Karl was one and the baby at the time. I have been blessed to witness all their infant moments and growth into young men. I specifically recall, shortly after Chris was born, Sister Cheryl making her hair appointment with my wife. She would have Chris with her. She could be seen reading her Bible and comforting Chris at the same time. As the boys grew, I would notice certain things that caught my attention. They were happy kids. Charles would cling to his mom, and I would chuckle. He understood stranger danger at an early age. Karl and Chris were typical boys who loved to have fun. On some occasions I would update Pastor after I would see his family. Of all the things he and I talked about, the topic of me seeing them brightened his day the most.

It was made known to me on the new organizational chart that a different reporting relationship would exist for the department and me. I reported directly to the new police chief, even though I still held the rank of deputy chief. In the past, the internal affairs chief reported to the assistant chief. As one would imagine, I was curious. Many within the police department were also curious about the new reporting dynamic.

After returning from the FBI Academy, where I had been receiving training for several months, I met with the new chief to receive the charge for my new assignment. He was pleasant, and he outlined the objectives he had in mind for internal affairs. He relayed that based on feedback he received from the community, he knew he could trust me.

I reached out to Pastor Wesley shortly after my meeting and told him in private about my experience. Pastor prayed for me, encouraged me, and assisted me in my new position. Among the many gifts God had given Pastor Wesley, he was especially adept at forecasting Satan's attacks.

To make it plain, Pastor seemed to always be a step ahead of them.

I continued to serve as the internal affairs chief. It was a good learning assignment that prepared me for what God already had planned.

Shortly after the birth of my two daughters, I was notified to report to see the chief. This call was unusual, as I would normally brief him during the early part of the week on what officers were doing and who was being investigated. As I reported to the meeting, I recall wondering if someone had done something that required me to start an investigation. When the chief saw me outside his office, I recall him calling my name out in a loud, joyful spirit. I said to myself, *Thank you, Lord! It doesn't seem like trouble.*

He informed me in private that the highest ranking African American chief was retiring and that I was his choice to succeed him. I was excited to receive such confidence from the chief, but understood through our dialogue that the plan he was proposing would rid the African American community of a long, hard-fought gain of having a three-star chief, which had been the case for less than one year. Specifically, he wanted to promote me to a two-star position initially, and one year later promote me to the three-star position. The chief then offered another option, which could have caused a fracture within the community, as well as within the department.

I thought about the matter and prayed for days as I was ordered not to talk about it to anyone for obvious reasons. I leaned on God and found comfort in Proverbs 3:5–6. I trusted God and later decided to make a phone call. Guess whom I decided to call? Pastor Wesley! After speaking of every scenario he and I could come up with, he never recommended a certain course of action. He knew I had to live with any decision I made. As we often did, we prayed. I declined the promotion and later told Pastor of my decision.

Soon thereafter, I was still promoted to a two-star chief position, although not the one we had earlier discussed, and I was assigned to command three of the city's six patrol divisions, one area being Oak Cliff. I reached out to Pastor Wesley to update him. He was pleased and expressed his continued support. We met often as Dallas was continuing to move at a breakneck pace. After these events unfolded and some time passed, the chief announced his resignation.

The Dallas Cowboys had just won the Super Bowl, and a parade was in order. The parade resulted in violence and chaos, with city officials personally witnessing it. It turned out to be problematic for the city and caused a strain on its image. The blame game ensued. It resulted in a lack of confidence within the command structure within the police department. With the existing circumstances, a nationwide search was conducted. A new chief from Phoenix, Arizona, was hired, and after six years, he retired. Pastor Wesley and I spoke regularly during this time.

During the late 1990s, my family and I joined Antioch Fellowship. We have loved every moment and thank God He allowed us to become members. Pastor Wesley approached me in 1999 and spoke with me about becoming a deacon. I was overjoyed! My reputation was intact, and it was confirmed by Pastor Wesley's designating me to become a deacon, along with others. After months of training, we became deacons on a Sunday evening.

The following week, the city approached me and asked me to become its first African American police chief. I accepted and was told to keep the announcement a secret. After the secret period had passed for anyone other than my wife, guess whom I called? Pastor Wesley! He received the first call.

Pastor Wesley was excited and happy about the announcement. I requested that he immediately come to city hall, if possible, to stand by my side. Pastor made it in time to pray with me before we proceeded to the podium.

Pastor Wesley spent several hours with me that day. He took interviews attesting to my character. While people knew me throughout Dallas, it was comforting that my pastor could communicate how God had blessed me. Pastor didn't need to have talking points, because he had walked on this Christian and professional journey with me for more than a decade before I was appointed police chief.

Pastor Wesley's contribution to the city of Dallas is without measure. He worked tirelessly to help those who couldn't navigate the stormy waters of life. He strategically directed his efforts for God's program with laser focus. He lifted men and women by proclaiming God's Word. He lived a life reflective of how God would want all of us to live.

When I became chief, the average tenure for a police chief within a major city was two and a half years. God blessed me to make almost four years. I would have preferred more time as police chief, but it wasn't in God's plan. We all know how hard Pastor Wesley fought for my reinstatement.

I am reminded of a night I laugh about currently. Pastor Wesley loaded many of us up in buses, and we proceeded to protest at the state fair over my termination. As we were protesting, our Dallas county commissioner, John Wiley Price, arrived in his personal car. We were actually blocking his entrance. I thought about all the days I was deployed by former police chiefs to ask Commissioner Price to go home from protesting so traffic could flow. God knew I needed a laugh at that exact moment. By the way, Commissioner Price was always a friend and true supporter. No shade on him in any way.

I was almost overcome with emotions when Chris was answering questions before the deacon ministry in February. I actually spoke about how his dad, Dr. Karry D. Wesley, fought for justice in Dallas. The night I spoke about it, Chris reminded me that he was there, too, "wearing my T-shirt." It was touching.

Dallas will always remember Pastor Wesley and his efforts to make Dallas a better place to live. I am forever grateful for his sacrifices and humble spirit. I find great joy in the times Pastor and I spent on this Christian journey together. His legacy will continue to live on.

45

My Pastor, My Brother, My Friend

BRENDA MOSBY

PASTOR WESLEY AND I started our business relationship back in 1995 when he purchased his first vehicle from Powell Chevrolet, and the Wesley family have been Chevy-GMC customers ever since. He strayed away once, and I still remember his call. "Brenda, I think I want an Escalade—Cheryl likes it," he said. I sent Pastor over to a Cadillac dealership to pick out the one he wanted. After he picked it out, I had the salesperson deliver the Escalade and paperwork to him at the church.

Pastor was a loyal customer and knew without a shadow of a doubt he was going to be taken care of in sales and service. That's why when Chevrolet asked for my recommendations for a prominent individual in the community worthy to carry the 2002 Winter Games Olympic Torch Relay when it passed through Dallas, Texas, the only person who came to mind was my pastor, Dr. Karry D. Wesley. He carried the torch in the relay that year and made national history.

My relationship with Pastor began moving toward brother and friend about fifteen years ago. I walked out of the dealership, and there stood my Pastor on the service drive waiting for the courtesy van to give him a ride. I asked him to give me a minute, and I went back inside. I admit, I was not happy. I went to his service advisor and said, "Pastor Wesley can drive any vehicle on this lot. Don't ever send him home in the courtesy van again!" That day I witnessed Pastor as a real living example of a humble and unpretentious man. That day I was more humbled, and it was the beginning of our personal relationship as brother and friend.

Over the years, I could always call and depend on my brother and friend. His warm and kind spirit always had a word of guidance and encouragement for me and my family. There have even been times when a coworker at the dealership was in need of an ear and voice of encouragement, and Pastor Wesley answered the call with no questions.

There is no way for me to reflect on Dr. Karry D. Wesley in a few words. I could go on and on. He was special to me and my family. The truth of the matter is that the legacy of my pastor, brother, and friend will live on in my life and in the lives of my family. I will always be there for the Wesley family.

46

A Safe Place

DEBRA BOWLES

Pastor Wesley was a man who truly listened to the Spirit of God and delivered the Word. He moved as a true steward of the gospel ministry, and he oversaw a filled congregation and the communities he served. When I speak of such a great man as Pastor Karry D. Wesley, this passage comes to mind:

> "For I was hungry and you gave me something to eat, I was thirsty and you gave me something to drink, I was a stranger and you invited me in, I needed clothes and you clothed me, I was sick and you looked after me, I was in prison and you came to visit me."
>
> Then the righteous will answer him, "Lord, when did we see you hungry and feed you, or thirsty and give you something to drink? When did we see you a stranger and invite you in, or needing clothes and clothe you? When did we see you sick or in prison and go to visit you?"
>
> The King will reply, "Truly I tell you, whatever

you did for one of the least of these brothers and sisters of mine, you did for me." (Matthew 25:35–40 NIV)

Pastor Wesley was that brother, friend, and leader. When women and children who were hungry and needed a safe shelter ran from violence and violent circumstances, by God's grace and love, Pastor Wesley was always there. His love, leadership, and concern were always seen by those who needed a place of refuge. I knew his service was genuine, and the survivors of Women Called Moses who have been served greatly benefited from his efforts.

Many people are not aware that when I first began my ministry, I had relentlessly reached out to many in our community, but to my overwhelming disappointment, I had received little or no support. It was rough in the beginning, but one day in 1998, by the grace of God, I was led to Pastor Wesley and the Antioch family. Pastor Wesley, along with his congregation, locked into a lifelong partnership with our ministry, and he helped me to continue this much needed stewardship in our community.

In closing, many people preach the gospel, but few are the gospel. Pastor Wesley was a true example of the living gospel. I believe that on this day he continues to be a beacon of light and good news to all. His work and legacy will continue to live on. He didn't just fight the good fight, but he also won the fight by leaving a living testimony within all the people he touched and saved. Job well done to our friend and brother, a great and faithful servant of God!

47

He Showed Up!

WILLIS JOHNSON

KARRY DON WESLEY WAS introduced to me in 1992 by Denny Davis as we started the Bishop Five. The purpose of the Bishop Five was to be supportive of Paul Quinn College, and that we were, but a bond was formed with the five to the tune that they were part of my marriage ceremony to my wife, Sophia, in 2010.

A very special bond was formed while we did the Bishop Five Revival from 1992 to 2002 at the Friendship West Baptist Church. We raised three million dollars, but the revival became "the revival" for the city of Dallas. People came from all over to attend, and during that ten-year period, I watched the five churches grow in size from regular to mega. Antioch Fellowship stands today as one of the most respected churches in Texas because of Pastor Karry Don Wesley.

We worked not only for Paul Quinn College, but also for other community issues that came to the forefront, like payday loans, economic development of the southern sector, and domestic abuse in Dallas—in all these, when I asked Pastor Wesley for his help, he showed up every time.

We all have had our issues with life and the ups and downs that come with it. When I was personally at a very low moment in life, I got a text from Karry that said, *In a season of character assassination, know that I am your friend and read Psalms 46:10.* It came at a time when I needed it the most, and it was such an encouragement. But that's who Karry was. He was no-nonsense and had very tight parameters, but he was loyal, and you could always count on him.

On the morning of November 13, 2019, I sent Karry a text that he had previously sent me. I did it at 8:40, and I am told that he died two hours later. Of course he never responded to my text, but in my spirit, I felt it. He and I last saw each other on September 28 at the church as we were doing a community event. He and I talked about our battles with cancer, and he was clearly in the best of health (so he thought). His conviction to God and his family were stronger than ever.

It is such a loss to this community, but that is selfish of us as a city because Cheryl and the boys are without a husband and father, and clearly his commitment to them was unmatched. Karry will be missed in his presence, but not in his spirit.

Karry, you are my friend, and I still read Psalm 46:10 today, just as you told me in August 2011.

What a man!

Co-Laborer and Friend

DR. ANTHONY SHARP

Dr. Karry Wesley, a brother, co-laborer, friend, colleague, and preacher par excellence. It's my contention that every now and then God purposely places people on your path who push and pull you to give God your best in service. I thank God for the years that I had the privilege of sharing the gospel of grace alongside Dr. Wesley and the other brothers who comprised the Bishop Five. Many lives were influenced and impacted for the greater good because Dr. Wesley was not ashamed of the gospel. He fleshed out his convictions concerning our Christ in word and deed. I trust and pray, long live the legacy of Dr. Karry D. Wesley.

A FINAL WORD

MUCH HAS BEEN SHARED about the man Karry Don Wesley. You've read of his childhood antics, his Christian conversion, his belief in education and excellence, his quiet yet wise demeanor, and his demonstrative love for his family, the people of God, and justice for all. More importantly, you heard of his love for the Lord, who saved him and used him for His glory. He lived the gospel!

There are many others all over the country and world who, if given the opportunity, could have shared what Karry Don Wesley meant to them. Neither time nor space allowed it to be, yet we know that his work of sharing the love of Jesus Christ through word and deed will live on in the hearts of people for years to come.

My husband died of gastric cancer. During his season of illness and treatment, we were experientially made aware of the expense associated with health care. Fortunately for him, he had excellent coverage, but there were others who did not. Patients had to pay out of pocket for extensive testing, physician bills, prescription medications, and hospital stays. Add to this the cost of transportation and the emotional and mental challenges of being sick. Often exhausted from treatments, many couldn't adequately take care of their personal hygiene nor cook and clean for themselves. Why do I mention this? Because there is something we can all do to honor the legacy of my husband.

In your own community, look for those who are in need of assistance, and offer it.

- Provide transportation to and/or from physician appointments, or pay for it.
- Give financially to assist with medical costs and prescription medications.
- Cook for or have food delivered to the patient on their treatment days.
- Offer to clean or pay for a cleaning service to assist one day a week or month.
- Help ensure patients are connected with other available resources.

We will be providing these services and more through a foundation honoring the legacy of Karry Don Wesley:

The Wesley Legacy Group, LLC
Website: wesleylegacygroup.com
Email: wesleylegacygroup@outlook.com

All profits from the sale of this book will go to the benefit of others.

The Wesley Family sincerely appreciates your love and support in this season. Our prayer is that Our Lord will bless and keep you in His care.

Order Information

To order additional copies of this book, please visit
www.redemption-press.com.
Also available on Amazon.com and BarnesandNoble.com
or by calling toll-free 1-844-2REDEEM.